DATE DUE

AP 07 MY 1 01			
FE 3 04			
JY 2 8 05			
AP 7 07			
MY 1 4 07			

DEMCO 38-296

Public Opinion, the First Ladyship, and Hillary Rodham Clinton

WOMEN IN AMERICAN POLITICS
VOLUME I
GARLAND REFERENCE LIBRARY OF SOCIAL SCIENCE
VOLUME 1074

WOMEN IN AMERICAN POLITICS
BARBARA A. BARDES, *Series Editor*

PUBLIC OPINION, THE FIRST
LADYSHIP, AND HILLARY RODHAM
CLINTON
Barbara Burrell

Public Opinion, the First Ladyship, and Hillary Rodham Clinton

Barbara Burrell

Garland Publishing, Inc.
New York and London
1997

Library of Congress Cataloging-in-Publication Data

Burrell, Barbara C., 1947–
       Public opinion, the first ladyship, and Hillary Rodham Clinton /
       Barbara Burrell.
              p.   cm. — (Garland reference library of social science ; v. 1074.
       Women in American politics ; v. 1)
       Includes bibliographical references and index.
        ISBN 0-8153-2142-2 (alk. paper)
          1. Clinton, Hillary Rodham—Public opinion.   2. Presidents' spouses—
       United States.   3. Women in politics—United States—Public opinion.   4. Sex
       role—United States—Public opinion.   I. Title.   II. Series: Garland reference
       library of social science ; v. 1074.   III. Series: Garland reference library of
       social science. Women in American politics ; v. 1.
       E887.B87   1997
       973.929'092—dc20   96-29385
                                                                                              CIP

Cover illustration of Hillary Rodham Clinton courtesy of The White House.

Printed on acid-free, 250-year-life paper
Manufactured in the United States of America

Contents

Illustrations   vii

Acknowledgments   ix

Chapter 1. Introduction   3

Chapter 2. Public and Private Domains and Political Wives   9

Chapter 3. The Campaign for the White House   25

Chapter 4. Public Perceptions of the First Lady   45

Chapter 5. The First Lady and Public Policy Making   87

Chapter 6. Personality and Political Leadership   117

Chapter 7. Conclusion: The First Lady and Equality for Women   135

References   149

Index   161

Illustrations

Figures

3.1 Average Favorable and Unfavorable Ratings, Hillary Rodham Clinton, 1992 Campaign   35

4.1 Favorability Ratings for Hillary Rodham Clinton 1993   47

4.2 Trend in Favorability Ratings for Hillary Rodham Clinton 1994   48

4.3 Unfavorability Ratings for Hillary Rodham Clinton 1993   49

4.4 Unfavorability Ratings for Hillary Rodham Clinton 1994   50

4.5 Average Favorability/Unfavorability Ratings for Hillary Rodham Clinton 1993   52

4.6 Average Favorability/Unfavorability Ratings for Hillary Rodham Clinton 1994   53

4.7 Average Favorability Ratings for Hillary and Bill Clinton 1993-1994   56

4.8 Favorability Ratings for Hillary Rodham Clinton by Sex   65

4.9a Favorability Ratings for Hillary Rodham Clinton by Party   67

4.9b Unfavorability Ratings for Hillary Rodham Clinton by Party   68

4.10 Favorability Ratings for Hillary Rodham Clinton by Sex and Party   69

5.1 Public Opinion of the Amount of Hillary Clinton's Influence in the Clinton Administration   98

5.2 As first lady, do you think Hillary Rodham Clinton has too much power, about the right amount of power, or too little power?   99

Tables

3.1   Multivariate Analysis of Group Support for Hillary Clinton   39

4.1   Hillary Rodham Clinton's Favorable Ratings in the States   60

4.2   Favorable Ratings for Hillary Clinton and Hillary Rodham
        Clinton by Region, Spring 1994   62

4.3   Multivariate Analyses of Group Support of Hillary Rodham
        Clinton, by Quarters of the Year, 1993-1994   71

4.4   Multivariate Analyses of Feeling Thermometer Scores
        and Sociodemographic Variables, Post 1994 Election Survey 73

4.5   Multivariate Analyses of Sociodemographic and Attitudinal
        Variables and Support for Hillary Clinton, Southern Focus
        Poll, Spring 1994   75

4.6   Multivariate Analyses of Feeling Thermometer Scores
        and Sociodemographic and Attitudinal Variables, Post 1994
        American National Election Survey   77

5.1   Multivariate Analyses of Group Support for the First Lady's
        Involvement in Policy Making   106

6.1   Personal Qualities—Percent Who Agreed   122

6.2   Multivariate Analyses of Demographics and Opinions of
        Hillary Rodham Clinton's Personality   125

Acknowledgments

This project began as a roundtable presentation on Hillary Clinton at the 1993 Southern Political Science Association annual meeting. Professor Mary Guy of the University of Alabama invited me to participate in this venture. Not being a scholar of the First Ladies but rather of women candidates for public office I was concerned about what I could offer in the way of an intellectual perspective on this person and position. But also being a student of public opinion, I decided to explore what the people were thinking about Hillary Clinton as First Lady based on polling data. Because she had been controversial and was attempting to take the First Ladyship in new directions, I found more public opinion data than I ever imagined available on her, giving at least one view of the people's response to her. The result is this book.

In gathering the data upon which this book is based, I was very dependent on the generosity and interest of others in the public opinion polling community. This book would not have been possible without the sharing of data by several national polling firms and academic survey research laboratories. I wish to thank David Krane of the Harris Poll, Lydia Saad from the Gallup Poll, Celinda Lake and the Terrance Group, and the Times Mirror Publishing Group. Beverly Wiggins at the University of North Carolina's survey research laboratory was very helpful in getting me started on my search for public opinion polls. Robert Cioe and Kathleen Frankovic from the *Los Angeles Times* and CBS News respectively provided me with crosstabulations on group characteristics and support for Hillary Rodham Clinton. Laura Guy and her staff at the Social Science Data Library at the University of Wisconsin-Madison were especially efficient and professional in obtaining data sets for my use.

Friends from around the country have made sure that I received clippings from their local newspapers on Hillary, providing me with perspectives on her with which to supplement poll data. Mary Stuckey, Mary Anne Borrelli, Diane Blair and Androula Lambrianidou have been particularly sensitive to my interests. Clyde Wilcox has e-mailed me whenever a *Washington Post* story appeared about Hillary. Plus, my husband and daughter called my attention to newspaper articles and stories on the nightly news at every opportunity. I appreciate their interest in this undertaking. I have been able to acquire a significant archive of articles on Hillary Rodham Clinton because of so many people's awareness and support. In addition, Karlin Kohrs Campbell of the Communications Department at the University of Minnesota, who has also written on the

"Hillary Clinton phenomenon," read the whole manuscript and provided insightful comments for me.

Of course, the book would not be a reality without the enthusiastic and professional support of Barbara Bardes, editor of this series, and David Estrin, my editor at Garland Publishing.

Finally, I wish to thank the Wisconsin Survey Research Laboratory where I work as a researcher in charge of survey design. My colleagues have helped collect data on the President and the First Lady from the perspective of Wisconsinites and assisted me in analyzing data sets. Ben Kadel created the figures for this book and Barry Radler assisted in the proofreading of it. I hope they, too, are proud of the result.

Public Opinion, the First Ladyship, and Hillary Rodham Clinton

CHAPTER 1

Introduction

Perhaps it was inevitable that all of the debates, controversies, and conflicts that emanated from the contemporary women's rights movement about women's roles in society would eventually touch one of the most prominent, potentially influential, and yet most traditional positions women have occupied in the United States—that of First Lady. This occurred in 1992 with an explosion, as Hillary Rodham Clinton traversed the campaign trail on behalf of her husband's quest for the Presidency of the United States. She engendered, to put it mildly, a national discussion about the power and influence of women, and particularly of wives, in the political life of the nation. She made us think about and struggle with major questions of the relationship between private life and public life and gender politics.

After several years in the White House, she continues to be a contradictory symbol. To conservatives, she represents what is wrong with America, both in terms of the substantive national policies she advocates and her personification of the role of women; while liberals and, especially, feminists grapple with the idea of a woman in an unelected and unappointed position wielding political power as a senior adviser to the President. She has twisted all of the clear dividing lines between what political philosophers have considered the private domain (that is, wife, mother, and homemaker) and the public realm of power and influence in the civic life of a community. Of course, Hillary Rodham Clinton had not been primarily a homemaker prior to entering the White House; she had been a prominent professional who worked outside of the home. However, she does not come by her position in the White House because of her professional credentials but because of her relationship to a man. That is an old-fashioned way of exercising influence in contrast to those women who made headlines as candidates for public office in 1992 during the so-called "Year of the Woman in U.S. Politics."

A review of editorials and journalistic analyses during the election of 1992 puts the challenge Hillary Rodham Clinton presented to the American public in stark relief. For example, very early she became "a national Rorschach test on which Americans [could] project their views of gender and equality.... For some, she's an inspiring mother-attorney. Others see in her the overbearing yuppie wife from hell," according to a *U.S. News & World Report* report (Cooper 1992). Thus one ideological battle was framed as a clash between the professional and the homemaker roles of women. Hillary Rodham Clinton was characterized as "a new breed of political wife, representing a new generation of working women. To many she is a role model, an inspiration. In other quarters. . . [she] is seen as a brash, overbearing career woman one step away from being a liability. Her outspokenness has made many uncomfortable, even angry" (Hall, 1992). This clash was alluded to repeatedly in commentary on the campaign.

A second and very much related focus in the debate engendered by Hillary Rodham Clinton centered on the notion of the "First Lady" and what a person in that position should be like. There was a resistance and a questioning of "the idea of a First Lady openly engaged in the affairs of state... the public is still skittish about the idea of a First Lady who is more involved in substance than ceremony" (Dowd 1992). Some voters, "particularly older women are uneasy with the notion that Hillary is ambitious—not just for her husband, but for herself" (Clift 1992). Putting these two fault lines together in the political debate surrounding Hillary Rodham Clinton, i.e., women as politicians and wives as influential policy advisers, captures the problem for Americans.

The debate surrounding Hillary Rodham Clinton touches the core of the challenge the women's movement has presented to society. As historian Carl Anthony has described it, the "whole First Lady issue [is] a lightning rod for something that goes far deeper. And that is the hypocrisy we still have about the status of women. It is a jealousy" (as quoted in Morrison, 1992). Criticism of Hillary Rodham Clinton illuminated "society's ambivalence toward changing roles.... Men may be projecting on to Mrs. Clinton their hostility toward feminism, while women, overwhelmed by their multiple responsibilities, may be projecting their frustrations" (Pogrebin, 1992). But at the same time, many had a strong positive reaction to her; her defenders and champions were also vocal.

Why do we even have a First Lady? Part of the answer lies in the dual leadership role that the President fulfills. The President is both the head of the government performing executive and legislative duties and head of state who presides over ceremonial functions for the nation and represents the United States in the world. Most other democracies separate these two functions, some with a prime minister and a president. In this set of tasks, the spouse can serve as a substitute for the head of state for ceremonial functions and the family becomes a prominent symbol in national life, a sort of royal family. Because we do not have royalty, the "first family" becomes the focus of attention for the media, which link them with the public. Thus, the role of hostess has always been of prime concern to Presidential spouses (although some in the nineteenth century did not perform this "duty" for a variety of reasons).

The First Lady has the potential to become an important part of the Office of the President instead of simply assisting with ceremonial head-of-state duties as a staffing system around the President has grown and the public role of women has enlarged. Certainly Hillary Rodham Clinton has had a larger vision of the First Ladyship. Because the Office of First Lady could be transformed into an institutionalized policy-making center, a systematic analysis of the people's beliefs about that office and the actions of the office-holder is an important part of the study of the contemporary Presidency and a significant indicator of gender politics in the United States.

First Ladies have always exercised private influence if they so desired. Some historically have been publicly influential, starting with the second First Lady, Abigail Adams. But moving toward a more formal notion of a role in policy making is a different step. The role of would-be First Ladies as more than cheerleaders for their spouses on the campaign trail did not begin with the 1992 election. In 1987, the Polk County Iowa Democratic Party sponsored a forum with the wives of six of the announced Democratic contenders for the Presidency. Each of the wives spoke about the issues that she would pursue in the White House and her vision of the role of First Lady. Such a gathering implied that voters should look beyond the man running for the office and examine the ideas of their spouses. It suggested an enlarged role and a policy prominence for future First Ladies. Interestingly, however, in her history of First Ladies, Betty Caroli concluded that the job of First Lady might actually shrink in the future. She thought that as more wives came to pursue their own professional careers, they would be less likely to drop them if their husband won the presidency (1987, p. 330). However, Hillary has rather expanded her position into one of a real political partner. In the first two years of her tenure in the White House, she experienced both successes and failures in her attempt to redefine the First Ladyship and, as the 1996 election approaches, remains a controversial figure.

Outline of the Book

Hillary Rodham Clinton has challenged the political system. The media, of course, have made much of this challenge to the traditional role of First Ladies in both political reporting and in commentaries as have Clinton's political opponents. The media have also sought to gauge the response of the public to her role and thus have commissioned public opinion polls to ascertain the reaction of the public. These polls are important. They tell us (with all of the caveats of polling methodology) how the people have been affected by this phenomenon and allow us to explore thinking about the interaction between the public and private in at least one aspect of gender politics.

This book uses the many and varied public opinion polls that have measured the people's reaction to Hillary Rodham Clinton and her activities to reflect on public acceptance or disapproval of this changing role for women. The chapters that follow tell the story of public response to Hillary as First Lady through a description and analysis of public opinion as measured in national and state surveys during the first two years of the Clinton administration. She has been the focus of polls from the early days of the campaign season. Never before has the public been asked so often what they think about a Presidential candidate's spouse and a First Lady. Not only have people's general responses to her as First Lady been surveyed but her different roles and aspects also have been explored—as policy advisor to the President and head of the Health Care Task Force, as an influential presence in the White House, her personal qualities and characteristics, her own future in politics, and her involvement in the Whitewater real estate deal while First Lady of Arkansas. I examine what these polls tell us about Hillary Rodham Clinton's relationship with the general public. Most importantly I ask what are the systemic implications of the public's response to this person in this position for the way that Americans think about women in political leadership roles.

We should expect a greater polarization in the people's response to Hillary Rodham Clinton than for most former contemporary First Ladies because of the image she (and the future president) developed during the campaign for the White House, which is discussed in Chapter 3. We should expect a greater intensity of feeling (both positive and negative) given the national discourse about her role in her husband's campaign and administration. Perhaps she has elicited distinctive responses from men and women—women being among her strongest supporters and men more challenged by her strength—because of the way in which she uses the role of wife in the public sphere.

Chapter 2 explores the development of the concept of public and private realms and what they have meant for women's position in society. It then presents an overview of the historical development of the First Ladyship with an emphasis on an examination of the First Lady's political influence. This discussion allows us to better evaluate Hillary's contribution to the development of the role of First Lady.

With Chapter 3 we begin to concentrate more centrally on the people's reaction to Hillary Rodham Clinton, focusing on the campaign for the White House in 1992. Chapter 4 then examines trends in support for and approval of her as First Lady in the major national polls. I discuss both methodological issues related to public opinion polling as well as substantive ones emanating from these surveys. I analyze group support for the First Lady (i.e., who has supported Hillary and who has been opposed to her) over time and consider the effect of Whitewater on her ratings. Both national surveys and state polls are used.

Chapter 5 explores the public response to the First Lady as policy advisor and their views of her influence. I consider personal responses to role and tease out more systemic reactions regarding women in politics.

Chapter 6 first considers the range of other questions that have been asked of the public about Hillary Rodham Clinton, especially questions about the quality and characteristics of her personality and about her future political leadership. To what extent do these opinions form a positive assessment and where do they suggest problems for women acting in political roles?

Chapter 7 summarizes the data and then makes linkages between the personal and political, the private and the public. It considers implications of this First Lady's transformation of the First Ladyship for women in politics and as political leaders in general.

My focus here is on the first two years of the Clinton administration. It was during this period that Hillary adopted a public policy advisory role to the President, and it is the public's response to this undertaking that I wish to address. At the end of those two years, her effort as head of the Health Care Task Force ended in a policy failure. Since that time, she has attempted to create a role for herself that fits the more traditional position of First Lady while not falling completely silent. The public's response to these latter efforts is not central to the theme of this work.

This study is complicated by the legal problems the Clintons have faced regarding work her firm did for the Madison Guaranty Trust. Special prosecutors and Congressional committees have kept the issue alive during the four years of the Clinton administration although it has risen and fallen in prominence over time. This problem has affected Hillary Clinton's ability to maintain a prominent role in policy making as First Lady as well as influencing people's opinion of her and of what the First Ladyship should be. Unfortunately, we cannot control for this feature of the administration in an assessment of people's response to her effort to transform the First Ladyship but have to take it into account and speculate about what the situation might be if the Clintons, and especially Hillary Clinton, had not been involved in this legal morass. Since Hillary Rodham Clinton undertook such a challenge to traditional ideas of a First Lady, her political opponents were able to use potential missteps made earlier in her career more forcefully than they might otherwise have been able to.

Finally, we need to keep in mind that any study of the Presidency or the First Ladyship cannot be separated from the individuals who have occupied those positions. Thus, Hillary's personality (and background) affects responses to her efforts, but my goal is an assessment of the First Ladyship as a public-policy advisory position within the Office of the President. Hillary's efforts are the instrument I use to undertake that goal. Thus, the issues are larger than this person in this role.

CHAPTER 2

Public and Private Domains and Political Wives

Theoretical and Historical Background

The division of the community into a public realm and a private realm is a socially determined construct. The private realm centers on home and family while the public realm is concerned with the making of rules for the community and the enforcement of those rules. Political philosophers established the public realm as the higher domain and assumed that only certain men should participate in that arena. Society constructed these divisions, confining women to the private realm because it was believed that women were incapable of performing competently in the public sector. Patriarchal societies were established, in which men dominated over women, and women were prohibited from speaking publicly. A central issue for feminists has been this division of the world into private and public domains and implications of this dichotomy for women's equality. They have sought to break women's silence.

The major assumptions of patriarchal society have been that men are naturally stronger, superior to, and more rational than women, who are naturally weaker, inferior in intellect, and unstable emotionally and thus are incapable of political participation. Men are destined to be dominant and act in the political world. They are responsible for and represent the polity. Women stand outside the polity. "Men by their rational minds, explain and order the world. Women by their nurturant function sustain daily life and the continuity of the species" (Lerner 1993, 4).

Aristotle laid the foundation for this philosophical development. He asserted that woman was "naturally" inferior to man. Woman was constitutionally unfitted for the highest good which was achievable only through involvement in public life. She was controlled by emotion, not by reason. According to Aristotle, the female's primary function was reproduction. She was to provide services and to carry out household tasks in order to free men to participate in public life. Silence was her glory.

Families and family life, while clearly inferior to public life, were considered the core of the community and necessary to allow those engaged in political life the freedom to participate in public activities (Okin 1979). For centuries, women were confined to the private sphere, viewed as inferior creatures and never given the tools, particularly education, to allow them to develop a sense of self and speak for themselves in the polity (Lerner 1993). In western political theory women were primarily considered in reference to domestic relationships, viewed only as wives and mothers. Aristotle's intellectual heirs in the eighteenth and nineteenth centuries even claimed that if women engaged in public speaking and other political activities they would damage their wombs (Jamieson 1988, 69). If they spoke, they would also threaten male dominance (Bardes and Gossett 1990).

In the revolutionary era in America, we find women energized by the quest for independence and active in the resistance to British rule. The economic boycott that American leaders used against Great Britain mandated the involvement of women because it "could succeed only if white housewives and their daughters refused to purchase imported goods and simultaneously increased their production of homespun" (Norton 1980). By the 1780s, women were "reading widely in political literature, publishing their own sentiments, engaging in heated debates over public policy, and avidly supporting the war effort in a variety of ways" (Norton 1980). As a result of the war effort, women struggled to conceive of a more political role for themselves, one that was compatible with their private duties. What emerged from this politicizing experience was the notion of "Republican motherhood" (Kerber 1980). "The Republican Mother integrated political values into her domestic life. Dedicated as she was to the nurture of public-spirited male citizens, she guaranteed the steady infusion of virtue into the Republic" (p. 11). In her new private role woman would not only provide physical sustenance to those engaged in the public life of the community, she would undertake the duty of developing political character in potential leaders and citizens. "The Republican Mother was to encourage in her sons civic interest and participation. She was to educate her children and guide them in the paths of morality and virtue" (Kerber 1980, 283). Thus, women could claim a significant political role, although it was to be played in the home. A consensus developed in the years of the early Republic "around the idea that a mother, committed to the service of her family and to the state, might serve a political purpose.... This new identity had the advantage of appearing to reconcile politics and domesticity; it justified continued political education and political sensibility [which women were seeking]. But the role remained a severely limited one; it had no collective definition, provided no outlet for women to affect a real political decision" (Kerber 1980, 283, 12). Citizenship was defined in gendered terms (Kerber 1995). The revolutionaries left intact the law of domestic relations which systematically merged the civic identity of women with that of their husbands. Husbands then controlled both their wives' bodies and their property. Married women had no will of their own (Kerber 1995).

After the Revolution women continued to be silenced in the public realm, but they began to challenge that silence. Beginning with the women's rights convention in Seneca Falls, New York, in 1848, women called for a more direct political role for themselves. That role eventually centered on obtaining the vote. Suffragists initially argued that equal justice demanded that women be given the vote. Their position was that "if all men were created equal and had the inalienable right to consent to the laws by which they were governed, women were created equal to men and had the same inalienable right to political liberty. In asserting that natural right applied also to women, the suffragists stressed the ways in which men and women were identical. Their common humanity was the core of the suffragist argument" (Kraditor 1965, 44). In her "Solitude of Self" address before the U.S. Senate Committee on Woman Suffrage (February 20, 1892), Elizabeth Cady Stanton argued that first a woman must be considered as an individual, then second as a citizen, third as a woman, and fourth as a mother and wife.

Later suffragists stressed differences rather than similarities between men and women as the basis of their rationale for wanting the franchise. They filled their speeches with suggestions that if women became political participants, private morality would override public immorality (Elshtain 1974). The suffragists in the age of Progressivism emphasized that if women were given the vote, reforms in government would occur. As activities once performed almost exclusively in the home became commercial activities, such as food and clothing production, they became the subject of legislation. Governmental regulation expanded. It was in women's interest to see that sound laws were passed and implemented in these areas so that they could be good housekeepers. "As the functions which they had previously performed as isolated individuals at home became social functions, women's claim to political equality changed from a demand for the right to protect themselves as individuals to an assertion of their duty to serve society as women. They assumed that their training as cooks, seamstresses, house cleaners and mothers qualified them to help in legislation concerned with food inspection, sweatshop sanitation, street-cleaning, and public schools" (Kraditor 1965, 68). Women should participate in lawmaking because government was now involved in large-scale housekeeping. The suffragists argued for the vote in order to better perform their duties as wives, mothers, and housekeepers. Progressive women reformers expanded the Republican Mother ideal as they "saw their commitment to honest politics, efficient urban sanitation, and pure food and drug laws as an extension of their responsibilities as mothers" (Kerber 1980, 284). For example, Jane Addams speaking to the National American Women's Suffrage Association in 1906 argued that:

> City housekeeping has failed partly because women, the traditional housekeepers, have not been consulted as to its multiform activities. The men have been carelessly indifferent to much of this civic housekeeping, as they have always been indifferent to the details of the household. The very multifariousness and complexity of a city government demand the help of minds accustomed to detail and variety of work, to a sense of obligation for the health and welfare of young children and to a responsibility for the cleanliness and comfort of other people. Because all these things have traditionally been in the hands of women, if they take no part in them now they are not only missing the education which the natural participation in civic life would bring to them but they are losing what they have always had (Buhle and Buhle 1978, 371).

Suffragists expressed little interest in greater direct involvement on the part of women in public affairs beyond obtaining the vote. They wished to use the vote to bring about public policy change but presumably did not see women as making these changes themselves as political leaders in public office.[1] They did not expect enfranchisement to lead to a radical redefinition of gender roles (Sims 1995). "Women would use the vote to change society, but the vote would not change women" (Elshtain 1972). That very much changed with the emergence of the second women's movement in the 1960s. Now women began to organize to achieve an equal role in government for themselves; women should not only participate in the election of political leaders, they should become leaders themselves. Contemporary feminists also sought to eliminate the rigid line between what was public and what was private. They have argued that "public and private could not be dealt with as

separate worlds, as if one exists in a rhythm independent of the other...
relations inside family and household are knocked into appropriate shape by
a battery of public policies" (Phillips 1991).

The National Organization for Women (NOW), the foremost women's
rights organization in the United States in the contemporary era, was founded
in 1966 to call for equal participation and treatment of women in
employment, education, and government. Task forces were established to
address issues of employment, education, religion, the family, the mass
media, politics, and female poverty in the range of relationships that would
be under attack.

Later, women in Congress would organize their own caucus to
promote issues of special concern to women.[2] A prime issue for the Caucus
has been the Economic Equity Act, which is a compendium of proposed bills
dealing with pensions and retirements, displaced homemakers,
nondiscrimination in insurance, child support enforcement, and care of
children and other dependents. Many of its provisions have been aimed at
homemakers and women on the bottom of the economic ladder (Burrell
1994).

Other organizations have formed with the primary aim of electing
more women to public office, but women have not been fully integrated into
political life because of the constraints of their private lives, particularly their
roles as wives, mothers, and homemakers. These constraints are both
psychological and substantive. As Sapiro (1983) has found, attitudes toward
equality and feelings of political efficacy among women are related to
marriage, motherhood, and employment. Only when women can earn as
much as men and have the same access to employment opportunities, when
they are not considered to be the primary child care givers and men are
integrated into the world of the home, will women be able to achieve an
integration into political life. Each aspect of women's private roles has
political significance and consequences that contemporary women's rights'
activists have articulated and attempted to make part of the public policy
agenda. Jamieson explains this dichotomy as a double bind that women are
striving to break out of (1995).

Public and Private Domains and the Role of First Lady

The idea of the First Lady in American politics joins in a unique way
the two domains of public and private life. This position has the potential
to dramatically alter the idea of what is private and what is public in the
political realm. The woman who serves as First Lady is there because of her

relationship to a man, not having attained a public position through her own achievements. She is to represent the expressive, supportive traditional role of women as wives, mothers, and homemakers. The word "First" suggests that she is to be a role model for others. "Lady," in this context, suggests a "certain kind of appearance, manners, and demeanor with connotations of middle-and upper-class respectability" (Mayo and Meringolo 1994). These expectations set up a conflict for First Ladies: as Presidents' wives, they are inevitably on the political stage; they take on a public persona, but as "ladies" they are expected to stay out of politics. (As women, they were not viewed as legitimately political creatures either.) Unelected and unappointed, the political influence of First Ladies is questioned. As women, their participation becomes suspect and controversial. It is these two aspects of the role—accountability and gender—that cause political and social stress.

The position of First Lady is full of cultural contradictions. Originally spouses were not publicly involved in electoral campaigns. Politics was outside of women's domain, plus it was viewed as a corrupt, dirty activity that would sully women if they became involved. But the President's spouse has evolved into an electoral asset to be used on the campaign trail. For example, the Republicans held "Pat Nixon for First Lady" week during the 1960 campaign, scheduling women's luncheons and coffees to win votes. On this campaign stage, however, the candidate's spouse was only suppose to urge people to become involved and support her husband, not to talk about public policy herself or to express her own views.

As White House hostess, the First Lady not only made people feel welcome but has made political statements with how and whom she entertained. Many First Ladies became quite adept at combining entertainment with advancing their husbands' political goals. The Smithsonian Institute exhibit "First Ladies: Political Roles and Public Images" provides an overview of this activity. Dolley Madison's entertaining, for example, had its political side as well as social. She "showed the skill of a candidate running for office, rarely forgetting a name or making an inappropriate comment" (Caroli 1987, 14). On the other hand, her successor, Elizabeth Monroe, was criticized and even caused a crisis in the Cabinet because she refused to perform the hostess role as it was defined in that era. First Ladies could also be advocates for public causes but only for certain types of issues in particular domains, "appropriate" issues that few would argue against, such as literacy and volunteerism.

Several books examining First Ladies' roles in historical context (e.g., Anthony 1990, 1991; Caroli 1987; Gutin 1989; Gould 1996), the creation of the permanent exhibit "First Ladies: Political Roles and Public

Images" at the Smithsonian, and numerous seminars and conferences in recent years have called our attention to the *political* history of the First Ladies. In this context, Hillary Rodham Clinton becomes the "latest in a long line of politically astute women who have been intimately involved with their husbands' political careers and administrations" (Mayo 1993). Her command and use of the position, however, as we will see, differs not only in degree from that of her predecessors but in its nature. "The fact is that Hillary Clinton has gone well beyond all her modern predecessors in her engagement in her husband's government. She may have the independent spirit of Betty Ford, shrewdness of Lady Bird Johnson, the seriousness of Rosalynn Carter, etc, down the line, but she is something different from all of these and more than the sum of their attributes. She is a strong, separate source of power inside the administration with a mandate of authority from the president and an operational base from which to carry it out" (Greenfield 1993).

Throughout the history of the Presidency, First Ladies have given political advice to their husbands and served as political confidants (some more than others). Abigail Adams, the second First Lady, was the first Presidential partner (and was severely criticized in the press for it, derisively called "Mrs. President"). Carl Anthony, who has perhaps most extensively examined the political roles of the First Ladies creates a picture of early Presidential spouses as very active in politics, often quite public about it and exerting a great deal of influence in Washington politics (Anthony 1990). They advocated public policy, were instrumental in political appointments, and sometimes served as messengers to and from the President. They were also subject to much criticism because of their public role.

First Ladies in the latter half of the nineteenth century, while focusing on the role of hostess, tended to exert private influence over political affairs, serving as advisers to their husbands behind the scenes. For example, Carl Anthony (1991) reports that "Many believed that Mrs. [Benjamin] Hayes secretly wielded a heavy magic wand over her husband's policies" and that "If [Caroline Harrison's] primary public role was exemplary goodwife, she was privately a political power... she knew her husband's stand on issues, and even promoted them by sending out copies of one of his speeches to Republican leaders."

In the early twentieth century, First Ladies "began to play more overtly political roles" (Mayo 1993), and the office of First Lady began to be institutionalized with the hiring by Edith Roosevelt of a "social secretary," the first salaried government employee answering to the First Lady as her boss (Anthony 1990, 295). Caroli characterizes the tenure of the first four

First Ladies of the twentieth century as altering "the meaning of the title they held. What had been unusual before 1900—the contribution of significant work of their own—became common among Presidents' wives" in the first two decades of the 1900s (Caroli 1987, 152).

The Influence of First Ladies

While some First Ladies have been influential in the public realm and acted as Presidential partners, the nature of their influence has varied. What historical precedents might Hillary Rodham Clinton have looked to in support of her activist public role? When historians have characterized First Ladies as being influential, they did not exclusively have in mind public policy decision-making. First Ladies' influence on Presidential politics has been of four types. One type of influence has involved directing and promoting a spouse's career, including climbing the political ladder. Helen Taft was a prominent practitioner of this type of influence. Among other things, she persuaded William Taft not to accept a Supreme Court appointment as it would preclude his being available for a Presidential nomination. Florence Harding, another First Lady adept at this type of influence, is quoted as saying "I know what's best for the President, I put him in the White House" (Anthony 1990, 393). These women's own ambition was advanced through the careers of their husbands.

A variant of this type of influence involved the protection of the health and well-being of one's spouse once he assumed the strenuous position of chief executive of the land (Caroli 1987). Caroli believes it was this latter type of influence that characterized Edith Wilson's sway over the White House as Woodrow Wilson lay ill in 1919 and 1920 rather than a desire to command over policy making. According to Caroli, Nancy Reagan's role during her husband's campaigns and presidency could be described in similar terms: "she saw her job as protecting him from overwork, inadequate staff, and poor scheduling.... This particular view of the role of a president's wife had very little to do with the kind of work he did, and should not be confused with the blatantly political roles that other women such as Helen Taft, Sarah Polk, Abigail Adams, and Rosalynn Carter took in their husbands' administrations" (1987, 150).

A second type of influence involved concern with and control over the social hierarchy of life in the Capitol. At times achieving this goal meant having a say over Presidential appointments, thus, indirectly affecting policy. Given that women were not allowed to exercise direct political power, their only outlet often became petty political intrigues around personalities. First

Ladies have been accused of having a keen interest in personnel decisions while in the White House often basing their "judgments on subjective or irrelevant considerations" (Caroli 1987, 132). Mary Todd Lincoln was a prime example. Or note, Helen Taft's comment regarding an appointment to her husband's Cabinet, "I could not believe you to be serious when you mentioned that man's name. He is perfectly awful and his family are even worse" (Gould 1985). Hillary Rodham Clinton's involvement in the dismissal of the White House travel office staff in 1993 would seem to fall into this domain rather than being a reflection of her transformation of the First Ladyship into a public advisory position.

A third type of influence concerned what was good for the President politically with the President's wife serving as political advisor, and a fourth type was a concern with public policy on the part of the First Lady. Abigail Adams set a precedent by being very much engaged in these latter two types of influence. Sarah Polk, an early Presidential spouse, was also very much the President's political and policy-making partner in the 1840s. She is even said to have remarked that if she went to the White House she would "neither keep house, nor make butter[3].... I always take a deep interest in State and national affairs" (Anthony 1990, 141).

While other First Ladies had acted behind the scenes in promoting public policy, Ellen Wilson broke new ground for a more substantial policy-making role for First Ladies, although she served only a brief tenure in the White House between 1913 and 1914 before dying. She took a prominent leadership position in housing reform in the early months of Woodrow Wilson's Presidency, starting an investigation of Washington's slums. Her name was attached to a slum clearance bill that Congress passed at the time of her death. It was the first piece of legislation passed with such direct and public assistance from a President's wife (Caroli 1987, 134).

Eleanor Roosevelt and Rosalynn Carter were even more active, testifying before Congress on behalf of their projects. Eleanor Roosevelt spoke about the concerns of coal miners and the people of the District of Columbia, while Rosalynn Carter testified on mental health concerns. Hillary Rodham Clinton would go one step further by assuming the lead before Congress regarding a major policy proposal of her husband's administration—health care reform. In this endeavor she has broken "the traditional expectation that the First Lady stay out of the political realm and not infringe upon the President's sphere" (Ryden 1993, 15).[4]

Hillary Rodham Clinton and the Role of First Lady

The nature and complexity of influence across the spectrum of First Ladies awaits further analysis especially as an historical link for Hillary Rodham Clinton's tenure in that position. She follows in a certain tradition while also being a path breaker. The image of Hillary Rodham Clinton has been one of a transformer of the position of First Lady. She came to the White House representing a new era, a new generation, the age of the professional woman, the smart woman. She would not exercise influence behind the scenes and then sit gazing adoringly at her husband when he was on stage. As the *Wall Street Journal* characterized her potential in December, 1992, she "promises to be something unique: both a major political power center in her own right, and the first modern working mother in the White House" (Frisby 1992). According to *The Economist* "[T]here has never before been a woman in the White House who had both a successful career and an independent powerbase before she arrived there.... She is a genuine trail-blazer" (December 5, 1992: 30). Clinton views herself as a transition figure (Quindlen 1994c). She promised to be an active, public "partner" in policy making. Clinton's philosophy is that the public and private are thoroughly interconnected. She thus violates the traditional separation of the masculine sphere and the feminine domestic sphere that has previously defined the role of First Lady (Ryden 1993).

Hillary Rodham Clinton does have historical predecessors for her active public role as suggested above, especially in Rosalynn Carter, who also headed her own commission and sat in on Cabinet meetings. (Although banned from legally being the chair of the President's Commission on Mental Health, it was her commission.) Indeed, a 1979 *Newsweek* cover story on Rosalynn as "The President's Partner" reads uncannily like an analysis of Hillary Rodham Clinton's first period in the White House. The First Lady is even referred to as Rosalynn *Smith* Carter in the story (emphasis added) (Morgenthau 1979). Perhaps, given changing views on women in society as the feminist movement grew and developed, Rosalynn Carter would have been credited with creating a more acceptable public policy-maker role for the First Lady had she not been followed by two first ladies who represented an earlier type of presidential spouse (and had Jimmy Carter been re-elected). But Hillary's predecessor for her very public policy-making position is more often said to be Eleanor Roosevelt than Rosalynn Carter. She herself has even stressed Eleanor Roosevelt as a role model.

Historian Doris Kearns Goodwin offered Hillary advice upon entering the White House from the lessons of Eleanor's tenure that will become significant as we explore the public's reaction to Hillary as First Lady. According to Goodwin,

> As you stake out your positions, some people will be angry with you. Thirty percent of the country probably thought Eleanor was the worst person ever to exist, a subversive agitator.... Although Eleanor engendered controversial feelings in some, at the same time she was an inspiration for others, particularly blacks but also young women, who saw her doing things women had never done before. The advice Eleanor would give you is: Don't worry about your public-opinion polls. Know that you're doing a good job when your friends respect you and your enemies are angry. One of the reasons Barbara Bush has had a 90 percent popularity rating is that she hasn't done anything. She may be warm and affectionate, but she won't leave any accomplishments behind. Don't feel constrained by polls, and don't worry about hurting your husband's political standing (1993).

First Ladies' Roosevelt and Clinton share similarities in how they shaped the position of First Lady even though important differences exist. They both have expressed a public commitment to policy concerns using their position as First Lady as a forum to call attention to national problems. Both have been the subject of criticism because of their political views. (See Goodwin 1993.) Each has been considered more liberal than their husbands.

Eleanor Roosevelt and Hillary Rodham Clinton have been perceived as role models for women seeking to expand their individualism and autonomy in society. But although Eleanor Roosevelt promoted greater equality and individualism for women, as a product of her time, she stressed a social feminism in keeping with a distinctive role for women in society and did not view women as equal with men in the world of politics. She supported protective labor legislation for women and opposed the Equal Rights Amendment being promoted by the Women's Party at that time. She did believe that women should be partners with their husbands first and homemakers second and that they should develop their own interests. She supported careers for women and spoke out on the right of wives to work. (See Caroli 1987.) Hillary, having the advantage of growing up in an age of increasing independence and expanding opportunities for girls and women, has stressed a more liberal feminism, seeing women as equal with men in all facets of life. Women's autonomy and independence are to be promoted. Women's roles are not particularly unique to liberal feminists.

Eleanor Roosevelt developed a career as a journalist after assuming the First Ladyship, although she had previously maintained her independence and had initially feared the First Ladyship might prevent her from having an autonomous existence. It was important to her to establish herself as a professional. In the opinion of her family, Eleanor Roosevelt wanted and needed a career to justify her own self-worth (Beasley 1987, 68). She, in part, achieved a peripatetic role in national politics because of her husband's limited ability to travel. She might have been kept more in the background and been forced into the hostess role of First Lady to a greater extent had polio not constrained the President's activities. However great her national influence, Eleanor Roosevelt was never part of FDR's inner circle of advisers, although some have considered her part of his "kitchen cabinet" (Caroli 1987). She acted as a gadfly in the administration and lobbied her husband along with others.

Hillary Rodham Clinton, on the other hand, had already established a professional career prior to entering the White House (that she had to downplay as would-be First Lady). She is also part of the President's inner circle of advisers and is considered a force in policy making. She plays a more central role than Eleanor did. However, after the failure of the Health Care Task Force which she headed, Hillary adopted a style more in keeping with that of Eleanor Roosevelt. She increasingly stressed the role of outside advocate and began a newspaper column that, while being policy oriented on occasion, also focused on the personal side of the White House. Eleanor had for years written a daily newspaper column called "My Day."

What has made Hillary Rodham Clinton's tenure in the White House a watershed is her representation of a new generation, and the fact that she is seen as a contemporary woman, the product of the feminist movement. As Goodwin pointed out "There's such a power base among women now that, if [Hillary] mobilize[d] them, [she would] be stronger than Eleanor ever was (1993). It is Clinton's relationship to the feminist movement that is crucial and makes the analyses undertaken in this book important. In her challenge to traditional expectations of First Ladies, she reconstructs their role through a fusing of the public and private (Ryden 1993).

She comes to her position at a time when women have redefined their roles and taken advantage of the changes in society that have resulted from the contemporary women's movement to expand their opportunities. Women are now the majority of college students, and while a "glass ceiling" still prevents many women from moving to the top in the business world, they are becoming doctors, lawyers, managers, and other professionals in greater numbers. When earlier First Ladies acted politically, they were depicted as exceptions or perhaps as curiosities. They might have been greatly admired, but they were not necessarily viewed as models for women in general.

There is greater significance to Hillary Rodham Clinton's actions. She has greater potential for altering the separation of private and public spheres in the sense that a private role may become a legitimate basis for public actions. One's role in the private sphere is not oppositional to performing a public role and being involved in making policy decisions for society. There is an intersection of what we think of as private and public. Her activism more generally focuses attention on women as political leaders. This is what is so unnerving to some and so full of potential to others. And the ambivalence about women's changing roles in our society has made the idea of an activist Hillary Rodham Clinton in the role of First Lady such an enigma.

What is distinctive in the role of First Lady is the use of the private role as a basis for participation in public policy making. The First Lady does not move out of the private realm into the public as have many women who have used experiences gained as wives, mothers, and homemakers as bases for community activity, which, in turn, has been used as credentials for seeking and holding public office. The First Lady meshes the private and the public realms and that merging may be accepted by the public as legitimate and the occupant of that position may be viewed as a political leader (as well as a most admired person). Of course, Hillary Rodham Clinton had been a public and professional person prior to the Clintons' quest for the White House, so to have expected her to serve only as White House hostess would have been unrealistic and naive. To use her own words, "The idea that I would check my brain at the White House door just doesn't make any sense to me" (Reed 1993).

For most of the contemporary feminist era, as more and more women have sought elective office and women's groups have organized to promote more women as lawmakers and chief executives, attempts have been made to neutralize stereotypes of women as politicians. Women tried to show that they could compete in a man's world and that the private world was irrelevant. In the 1992 election that strategy changed, most prominently when Patty Murray ran a successful campaign for the U.S. Senate in Washington State as "just a mom in tennis shoes." Her theme emerged from a put down by an opponent of her background. In 1994, however, female candidates for public office became proactive in promoting their private roles as not only a legitimate basis from which to launch a political career but as a positive context in which to run for public office. One should vote for them (among other reasons) because they were mothers. They promoted their motherhood with slogans such as "a Mom, not a millionaire" or "a mom with a mortgage." People were supposed to vote for them precisely because they were mothers and had had certain experiences that their opponents had not had. Out of these experiences, they believe, have come perspectives important to bring to the policy-making process. One candidate, for the U.S. House of Representatives, Zoe Lofgren, even went so far as to challenge the establishment by trying to put "mother" on the ballot as part of her job description. It was ruled not a legitimate job.[5]

The First Lady position still causes concern, however. Reflecting on Presidential candidate spouses, Campbell (1993) has noted that, "Women candidates ask voters to revise the relationship between women and public power. By contrast,... candidates' wives raise the more problematic issue of the relationship between women, *sexuality*, and power. That is, spouses exert their power by virtue of their sexual and marital relationship to the candidates; their influence is indirect and intimate, a subtle intrusion of the private into the public, political sphere" (p. 1). This is most threatening to men who have viewed the home and their homemaker-wives as a refuge from the world of economic and political power. If a woman can exert influence through her private role as spouse without being part of the labor force or holding a formal position in the public realm, this dramatically challenges relative positions and power structures in society.

The problematic issue is one of gender and position (and implications for power) or what used to be called derisively "petticoat government." It is the particular nature of combining the personal and the political. As one journalist posed the problem "Why does the prospect of Hillary Clinton as attorney general bother some of us more than the reality of John Kennedy's brother?" (Pollit 1993). Why is the idea of wives of political figures wielding power on their own so unsettling to Americans, even to political liberals? (Unelected advisors are part of any administration.) Feminists, too, seemed to be uneasy about Hillary Rodham Clinton's role as First Lady rather than as presidential candidate at least as intimated by the media. One has to achieve on one's own to be a legitimate actor in the public realm. It is part of the individualistic culture of American society.

The feminist movement sees political wives as becoming independent actors able to pursue their own interests and careers rather than being constrained to play the supportive spouse and political hostess roles in furtherance of their husband's careers. But political spouses like Rosalynn Carter and Hillary Rodham Clinton, rather antithetical to the prescription of the movement, have used their relationship with their spouse to achieve influence instead of seeking their own identity. (See Greenfield 1977.)

The idea of First Lady in the political process, then, is full of complexity. First and foremost is the issue of gender. It matters that we are talking about *women* in this role for all of the historical and political theoretical reasons that have been cited. Second, and also very significant, is the fact that we are talking about a private and deeply personal relationship–marriage–that has public implications.　　Third, we are considering a traditional symbol, First Lady, an icon that has developed roles and images with great meaning for the public, that is being transformed. Fourth is the issue of accountability. If the person who serves in this role desires to be a political force, then how does the public hold her accountable for her influence? The First Lady has no formal position in the government. She receives no pay. She receives no confirmation from the U.S. Senate for her job. She cannot be fired. (She could be divorced, but that is a private matter.)　　Other advisers answer only to the President, but they can be dismissed. Ultimately, the First Lady is held indirectly accountable through the job her husband does as President.

Given the challenge Hillary Rodham Clinton has posed to the role of First Lady and the context of broad changes in women's lives that have occurred in the past quarter century, undertaking an analysis of her evolving relationship with the public is an important scholarly mission. I begin that mission with her odyssey through the campaign of 1992 and people's reaction to it as measured in the public opinion polls.

Notes

1. I intend to explore the extent to which the suffragists had a vision of women as political leaders in future work.

2. The Congressional Women's Caucus was founded in 1978 and became the Congressional Caucus for Women's Issues in 1981. In 1995, it, along with other "legislative service organizations," lost its right to use Congressional staff monies to support itself.

3. Had Hillary Rodham Clinton known about this comment, she might have been able to deflect with humor some of the criticism for her infamous "staying home and baking cookies" remark during the campaign of 1992. There is no evidence that Sarah Polk was chastised for such comments or for her involvement in public affairs.

4. From a contemporary perspective, we should also note Lewis Gould's characterization of Lady Bird Johnson's contribution to the development of a substantive role for First Ladies. According to Gould, "Working directly on legislation, rallying grassroots backing for national policy, Lady Bird Johnson demonstrated that a First Lady could now do more than serve as a feminine conscience or fact-finder of a Presidency. It was now conceivable that she could be a functional and integral part of the office itself" (1985, 535).

5. She won her primary anyway and the general election.

CHAPTER 3

The Campaign for the White House

Throughout Bill Clinton's tenure as governor of Arkansas, Hillary Rodham Clinton had been his political and policy-making partner. When he was defeated for re-election to the governorship after one term, she directed his comeback, even taking his last name as her own to placate irate Arkansas voters who viewed her as an "uppity woman." She often used the term "we" in describing the Clinton administration in Arkansas, and the Governor had talked in terms of "our" administration. She had acted as an "unpaid troubleshooter, marshaling expert opinion on an assortment of social issues. As the chair of Governor Clinton's Arkansas Education Standards Committee, she held public hearings in every county, helping build consensus for education reform" (Clift 1992a). She had also been the main wage earner in the family working as a law partner in the now infamous Arkansas Rose law firm. *The National Law Journal* had named her as one of the 100 most influential lawyers in the country. She had also engaged in a number of public service activities, most notably serving as chair of the Children's Defense Fund, and had been appointed to numerous corporate board directorships. Given her career and her resume, when Bill Clinton announced his candidacy for President, the stage was set for a dramatic change in the role of First Lady. How the Clintons introduced Hillary to the public, how the media framed this transformation, and how political opponents reacted would condition the public's response to a redefining of the First Lady as one of the President's policy advisors.

The Clintons initiated and encouraged the idea early in the campaign that Hillary would be a vital political adviser in the White House and play a prominent policy making role in a Clinton presidency. The aspiring President explained that if he were elected, "it would be an unprecedented partnership, far more than Franklin Roosevelt and Eleanor" (Sheehy 1992, 144).[1] He stimulated public speculation about an appointment for her to a Cabinet post. At fund raisers he would quip "Buy one, get one free." Hillary had said, "If you elect Bill, you get me." Thus, they promoted the notion of a dramatically different partnership to lead the country that the national media quickly picked up. For example, the *Detroit Free Press* heralded her unique position early in the campaign in a January 1992 story headlined "Some Say She's the One Who Should Be President" (Creager 1992).

Media Coverage

As Hillary Rodham Clinton established a prominent role in the Presidential campaign, she became the subject of innumerable press stories. She became the object of press scrutiny during the 1992 campaign to an extent not faced by any previous contemporary would-be First Lady. To say the least, she "engendered spirited public debate" (Cooper 1992). Headlines such as "The Hillary Factor," the Hillary Problem," "All Eyes on Hillary," and "Hillary Then and Now" led campaign news articles.

To establish a sense of the extent and range of coverage Hillary Rodham Clinton received during the campaign, I have surveyed a variety of data bases of media articles. Included in this process was the *Readers' Guide to Periodical Literature,* which indexes magazine articles, the Proquest electronic data base, and the *New York Times* and the *Washington Post* indexes.[2] What follows is not a comprehensive content analysis but rather an overview and illustration of media coverage. The Proquest search produced 234 articles under Hillary Clinton between January 1 and November 4, 1992. The focus of the earliest articles tended to deal with allegations of Bill Clinton's infidelity and Hillary's defense of him during the New Hampshire primary campaign. Some saw her as saving his campaign by her performance during a nationally televised interview on *60 Minutes* immediately following the Super Bowl in January. However, she also generated criticism from some quarters for her remark that she was "not sitting here, some little woman standing by my man like Tammy Wynette." Tammy Wynette took great offense at this comment, and Hillary was accused of being an elitist who had insulted country music fans. "Many country-western fans—there are millions—took the Wynette remark as an uppity slur on the music they love" (Benedetto 1992). "Mrs. Clinton's putdown of Wynette is only the latest example of why the Democratic Party has been losing the country-music vote in presidential elections" (Neal 1992). (See also Carroll 1992; Wooten 1992.)

Many of the early stories, however, focused on her being an asset to the campaign. For example, the *Chicago Tribune* headlined an article on January 31 "Hillary Clinton May Be Candidate's Top Asset" (McRoberts and

Thomas 1992). These stories were also initial acknowledgment that she would be a different type of First Lady. For example, in a Reuters News Service piece headlined "Stand by Your Man? New Look in Campaign Wives," Deborah Zabarenko described "Hillary Clinton as [stepping] forward as one of a new breed of presidential candidates' wives: smart, tough, telegenic and nobody's bimbo" (1992). Some reporters, however, had a difficult time figuring out how to describe the campaigning of this assertive political partner. One of the most mixed characterizations from this period was that of Joseph Kahn of the *Boston Globe*. In a February 13th piece titled "As her Husband's Campaign Struggles, She Hits the Hustings in New Hampshire," Kahn described Clinton as "[looking] less like the sweetheart of "60 Minutes" than a one-woman assault team, arriving by land, air and over frozen water to spray automatic-weapons fire on the Bush administration's domestic policies and political tactics.... Charismatic, articulate and accomplished in her own right, the 44-year-old Clinton is shucking the gloves this week and taking on her husband's opponents bareknuckled. To observe her up close during a full (very full) day on the stump is to understand why Arkansas folks are called 'razorbacks'—and why voters repeatedly ask her why she's not running for office herself.... On the battlefield of partisan politics, Hillary Clinton is not inclined to take any prisoners" (1992).

In March, the critical stories began in earnest primarily as a result of her "stay at home and bake cookies and make tea" comment (described more fully below). Discussion about her role and the role of political wives dominated the media during this time frame. In September of the campaign year, Robin Toner in the *New York Times* calculated that "At least 20 articles in major publications this year involved some comparison between Mrs. Clinton and a grim role model for political wives: Lady Macbeth" (1992).

As the campaign progressed and the Clintons headed to the July national convention, we began to get analyses of Hillary's political make-over in which she seemed to soften her rhetoric and her personal appearance and was showcased in more traditional contexts while attempting to play a more subordinate role to that of her husband. (Criticism of her for repositioning herself was also in evidence.) This emphasis continued through the Democratic convention in July. In August, media emphasis switched to coverage and analyses of the Republican attacks on her at their national convention. In the fall, the philosophical discussions about women politicians and political wives continued to a degree. Hillary Rodham Clinton also obtained coverage on issues and public policy as she gave a number of substantive speeches. She continued to counterattack the Republicans during this period.

Forty-one articles in 24 different publications appeared under the heading of Hillary Rodham Clinton in the *Readers' Guide* between January 1st and the election in November. They included three *People Weekly* stories with human interest profiles, highly critical pieces in the arch-conservative *The American Spectator*, and analyses by *U.S. News & World Report, Time,* and *Newsweek*. They included stories in "women's magazines": *Glamour* ("Are We Ready for a First Lady as First Partner?" and "Hillary Speaks to Her Mythologizers"), *Ladies Home Journal* ("Hillary Clinton: Road Warrior"), and *Vanity Fair* ("What Hillary Wants"), and the more feminist periodicals of *Working Mother* ("Hillary Clinton: Working Mom in the White House?") and *Working Woman* ("The First Lady with a career?"). The focus of these pieces can be roughly catalogued into six major areas: general analysis (primarily articles in the major news magazines), analyses with a feminist focus, negative analyses of her ideology and career, policy analyses (i.e., reviews of her writings and speeches—mainly positive in content), human interest pieces, and profiles. The purpose of cataloguing the general thrust of these articles is to illustrate the high interest she generated during the campaign and the variety of approaches and angles taken by the media. The distribution of each type of focus is as follows:

- 7 articles—general analysis
- 7 articles—feminist analysis
- 9 articles—negative analysis
- 5 articles—policy analysis
- 3 articles—human interest
- 9 articles—profiles

Her distinctive role in this election is further illustrated through a comparison of the number and type of articles about her with those about other Presidential candidates' spouses. Between January 1992 and November 4th, the *New York Times* listed 66 references in its index under "Hillary Rodham Clinton," 49 of which were under the subheading of "Presidential Election." This number compares with 33 references for Barbara Bush ("Mrs. George Bush"),[3] 17 of which were under the "Presidential Election" subheading.[4] Non-Presidential-election indexed articles concerning Barbara Bush primarily consisted of reports of trips and other activities as well as discussion of the President. The non-Presidential-election indexed articles under Hillary Rodham Clinton centered on issues such as "Children & Youth," "Child Custody & Support," and "Education and Schools," all dealing with her policy focus. Both women had citations under "Bakeries & Baked Products," and "Cookies." The *Washington Post* indexed 19 stories about Barbara Bush and 30 stories about Hillary Rodham Clinton during this same time frame.

The News Study Group at New York University tracked news coverage of Hillary Rodham Clinton from the campaign through her first months in the White House. They report that during the Presidential primary season when the story of Hillary Rodham Clinton was

> fresh and getting good play, male reporters were likelier to be writing about Hillary Clinton than female reporters (62 stories with male bylines, 58 with female bylines, 30 unattributed)[5].... The earliest coverage was likely to be conventional. Syndicated columnist and TV commentator Clarence Page, for example, wrote of the unwritten rules for spouses of political candidates in "Help for the Confused Political Wife" in the March 22, 1992, edition of the *Chicago Tribune*. Many early stories were also patronizing and/or hostile (according to Dick Williams of the *Atlanta Journal-Constitution,* Bill Clinton was "married to the radical Left"). In fact, press treatment of Hillary Clinton became a major story. The Clinton campaign, *The Washington Post* reported, was engaged in an "internal tug-of-war over how to divide Mrs. Clinton's policy-making and cookie-baking roles.... (Diamond, Geller, and Ruiz 1993)

Both male and female reporters have been accused of having a problem covering Clinton. Katha Pollit (1993) described what she viewed as the "Male Media's Hillary Problem" and Katherine Corcoran (1993) took on female reporters in her piece "Pilloried Clinton: Were the Women Who Covered Hillary Clinton During the Campaign Guilty of Sexism?" Pollit attributes the problem to ideological differences, jealousy, and "protection of turf." Male journalists are afraid of losing their jobs to women, she contended. Corcoran says that the "media were confused by Hillary Clinton. Reporters simply didn't know how to write about a post-women's movement, professional baby boomer in line to become first lady...."

But at least some in the media called attention to the larger issues about women's place in society involved in Hillary Clinton's campaigning, and thoughtful articles did appear discussing the contradictions and challenges emanating from her participation in the election. For example, the

New York Times referenced her as "a lightning rod for the mixed emotions we have about work and motherhood, dreams and accommodation, smart women and men's worlds," and the *Los Angeles Times* commented "The squirming over Hillary Clinton isn't so much about a First Lady as about ambivalence over women, power, work and marriage" (Morrison 1992). In "Time for a Feminist as First Lady?" Patt Morrison does a particularly insightful job of laying out the cultural tangles Hillary Clinton presented in the campaign. Overall, the media presented the public with a bewildering array of images and commentary from which to develop a perspective on the candidate's wife and to reflect on an evolving role for First Ladies.

Political Opposition

The political opposition attacked Hillary Rodham Clinton to an extent seldom experienced before by candidates' wives. Historically other First Ladies have been vilified after entering the White House. For example, during the Roosevelt re-election campaigns, foes chanted "We don't want Eleanor, either." But few have been the object of political derision as a would-be First Lady. Some Republicans had attempted to portray Kitty Dukakis as an unpatriotic radical in the 1988 campaign. And Andrew Jackson opponents "advised voters to consider carefully the wisdom of putting Rachel [Jackson] 'at the head of the female society of the United States'." Rachel Jackson's opponents' concern, however, was not her political beliefs but with her moral rectitude to serve as First Lady (Caroli 1987).

The Republicans launched an anti-Hillary campaign perceived to be so vitriolic that Bill Clinton accused them of trying to make Hillary Clinton the "Willie Horton" of the campaign. Writing in *Commonweal* in October, Abigail McCarthy (1992) reflected, "For good or worse, Hillary Clinton has been made an issue—the Willie Horton issue of 1992." (See, also, Mann's "Hillary Horton?" 1992). In perhaps one of the less biting of the criticisms, former President Richard Nixon warned that her forceful intelligence was likely to make her husband "look like a wimp." Voters, he told reporters, won't accept a man whose wife is "too strong and too intelligent" (*New York Times*, 2/6/92). Republican strategist Roger Ailes chimed in that "Hillary Clinton in an apron was like Michael Dukakis in a tank" (Hall 1992). At their national convention, she was shrilly attacked. Pamphlets depicted her as a "femi-nazi" (Lewis 1992). Patrick Buchanan denounced her as a champion of "radical feminism" and claimed that "Clinton & Clinton" would impose a far-left agenda on the nation" (*New York Times*, August 20, 1992). Richard Bond, chair of the Republican National Committee "caricatured Hillary Clinton as a law-suit mongering feminist who likened marriage to slavery and encouraged children to sue their parents" (Ifill 1992a). And Pat Robertson accused Bill and Hillary Clinton of "talking about a radical plan to destroy the traditional family and transfer its functions to the federal government" (Germond and Witcover 1993, 412).

The attacks perhaps reached their zenith in the national convention speech of Marilyn Quayle, which was viewed as going too far. The attacks backfired on the Republicans. According to Marilyn Quayle, "Not everyone [in her generation] believed that the family was so oppressive that women could only thrive apart from it." One line that made negative headlines was "They're [liberals] disappointed because most women do not wish to be liberated from their essential natures as women. Most of us love being mothers and wives." Just as Hillary Clinton earlier had been criticized for seeming to put down full-time homemakers, Marilyn Quayle appeared to attack women who had careers outside the home. Kathleen Hall Jamieson, Dean of the Annenberg School of Journalism at the University of Pennsylvania, found in a series of focus groups that the "essential natures" phrase was retained by women to a striking degree. According to Dean Jamieson, "The level of hostility toward [Marilyn Quayle] and that speech was very high. I think there was some resentment at someone standing up and telling women what choices are and are not appropriate for them" (Toner 1992). While this speech was an attack on liberals in general, it was widely viewed as an attack indirectly aimed at Hillary Clinton.

Hillary and the Campaign

How was it that Hillary Rodham Clinton became a controversial figure in the campaign? There were defining moments in the campaign for her, and for the most part they were not pleasant. Her main introduction to the public was the *60 Minutes* television interview in which she had to express support for and defend her supposedly philandering husband. That interview, although a very difficult and embarrassing situation, seemed to generate a positive response from the public, not withstanding the backlash over the Tammy Wynette comment.

But then her infamous "stay home and bake cookies" remark hurt. In response to a charge from Jerry Brown, a primary opponent of her husband's, that her law firm had benefited unfairly from her marriage to the governor of Arkansas, she commented "I suppose I could have stayed home and baked cookies and had teas." This line was widely quoted and seemed to be a put-down of women who had chosen to stay at home. It stroked the culture gap fires that had been a problem for the women's movement throughout its history. It "aroused hostility among traditional women who saw it as a condemnation of their life choices" (Campbell 1993, 4). (For a review of how this comment became a media issue, see Jamieson 1995.) However, this statement was only part of Hillary Rodham Clinton's response to Brown's charge. "I chose to fulfill my profession, which I had before my husband was in public life. The work that I have done as a professional, a public advocate, has been aimed... to assure that women can make the choices... whether it's full-time career, full-time motherhood or some combination," she had continued in the interview. The full context of her response suggests a more balanced reflection on the difficult decisions women have faced. But the media chose to ignore that.

The opposition also tore apart her earlier writings in law journals about children's rights. As several commentators have noted, however, this policy element of the debate engendered by Hillary Rodham Clinton on the campaign trail represented a turning point in commentary about First Ladies: she was not being criticized for her clothes or her social life but for her public policy stances. As Richard Cohen of the *Washington Post* put it "Something truly remarkable had happened. A spouse was being attacked not for the way she was dressed or (as with Nancy Reagan) where she was getting those dresses from, but for her views, for her writings, for her speeches..."(1992). As Suzanne Garment put it in the *Los Angeles Times*, "... there is something unusual about the criticism of Hillary Clinton. She is being attacked not for her character or her finances but for her views and positions. This, is, we must suppose, a step forward" (1992). Further, in a move "unheard of" for a prospective First Lady, Clinton was invited to a breakfast interview at the *Washington Post* where she was asked questions of a substantive nature (Corcoran 1993). Hillary Clinton had added a substantive focus to the campaign, however controversial, that citizens were able to reflect upon for the first time.

The People's View in the Campaign

Media attention given to the aspiring First Lady during the campaign included charting the people's impressions of Hillary Rodham Clinton through national surveys as her fortunes waxed and waned. The polls were often an integral part of the development of a story. For example, *Vanity Fair* commissioned a poll by Yankelovich, Clancy, Shulman for a major article by Gail Sheehy, a writer who had gained prominence writing psychological profiles of other national political figures. That poll included the public's general reaction to Hillary Clinton, whether she should pursue a separate career as First Lady, and a battery of items on her personal characteristics (Sheehy 1992).[6]

   U.S. News & World Report concluded as early as April, 1992 that their poll "show[ed] that Americans are sharply divided over Hillary Clinton. Forty-six percent of respondents say that she would make a good or excellent first lady... and that's well below the 77 percent who think Barbara Bush is doing a good or excellent job."[7] Near the end of the campaign, however, Donnie Radcliffe in the *Washington Post* concluded that "... the polls indicate she is no longer a liability to Bill Clinton; in a variety of surveys, her "negatives' are down from their startlingly high levels of the spring. She's no Barbara Bush, but she doesn't appear to be a drag on the ticket either" (Cooper 1992).

   How extensive were the polls during the campaign, to what degree did they show a public polarized in their opinion of Hillary Rodham Clinton, and to what extent was she viewed negatively? What did they indicate about her base of support and opposition? The earliest poll, one conducted by Yankelovich in February, not surprisingly found that the majority of the public had not yet formed an opinion. Sixty-five percent said they were either unfamiliar with Hillary Clinton or unsure of their opinion. Twenty-six percent had a favorable opinion and 9 percent were unfavorable.   By March, Gallup (for *USA TODAY*), CBS/NYT and the *Washington Post* had all begun to ask the public about its impressions of Hillary Clinton. CBS/NYT and the *Washington Post* found 31 percent and 28 percent, respectively, having a favorable opinion while 17 percent and 22 percent, respectively, had a negative opinion. A majority had no opinion in the *Washington Post* poll. Gallup reported a more highly crystallized opinion base: 39 percent were favorable and 26 percent were unfavorable in March of 1992. By April, Yankelovich found negative impressions doubling to 19 percent from the 9 percent he had found in February, while favorable impressions dropped one point to 25 percent. Another poll at the end of March shows something quite different. *Newsweek* had commissioned the Gallup organization to do a national poll. The results were reported in a sidebar to a March 30 article titled "Will Hillary Hurt or Help?" In this poll people were asked, "What is your overall impression of Hillary Clinton, Bill Clinton's wife: favorable or unfavorable?" Sixty-five percent said "favorable" and 16 percent responded "unfavorable." This is an extraordinarily high rating hardly suggesting that Hillary had become a liability to the campaign. But nowhere in the article are the poll results discussed. The article states, however, that "The core issue, arguably, is whether America is really ready for a self-confident, politically active woman like Hillary Clinton as First Lady" (Carroll 1992, 31). That poll seemed to have answered that question in the affirmative for the moment.

Given that voters usually do not focus their attention on the campaign for the Presidency until the fall of the election year (although their opinions are extensively measured from the earliest days of the campaign), these polls do show an unusually fast decline in respondents expressing "no opinion" on this future First Lady. Figure 3.1 shows average favorable and unfavorable ratings for Hillary during the 1992 campaign months across the available polls.[8] Her highest favorable ratings were the 65 percent obtained in the Gallup Poll for *Newsweek* cited above and in September when 56 percent expressed a favorable opinion of her. Her highest negative rating was 33 percent obtained in the *U.S. News & World Report* April survey.

Generally about one-third to 40 percent of the public had a favorable opinion, and about one-fifth to one-quarter had an unfavorable impression of Hillary Rodham Clinton during the campaign. The only comparison we have from previous Presidential elections is an October 1988 poll done by NBC on Barbara Bush and Kitty Dukakis. In that poll, 48 percent of a sample of likely voters had a favorable opinion of Barbara Bush, 11 percent were unfavorable and 41 percent were unsure. Kitty Dukakis was viewed favorably by 42 percent, unfavorably by 11 percent, and 47 percent were unsure of their opinion of her. Thus, positive opinions of Hillary compared favorably with these previous candidates' wives, but her negative ratings also were somewhat higher. Because of her prominent position in the campaign, people were more familiar with her and had more definite opinions about her than they had had regarding previous candidates' wives.

The polls were not the only sense of public opinion that politicians had about Hillary Clinton during the campaign. She was also the subject of focus groups conducted by both sides in the campaign and by a dial group the Clinton campaign used.[9] The dial group in the spring of the campaign showed that Hillary was not helping the campaign. "The readings fell precipitously at the mere sight of her face on-screen" (Goldman et al. 1994: 255). In the focus groups, as reported by Clinton's pollster Stan Greenberg, "people [thought] of her as being in the race 'for herself' and as 'going for the power.' She is not seen as particularly 'family-oriented.' More than Nancy Reagan, she is seen as 'running the show'" (Goldman et al. 1994: 251).

In an April 27 report, Clinton advisers wrote that "Hillary should have a lower profile in the immediate short-term, as we try to reintroduce Bill Clinton.... After a short pull-back period, Hillary needs to come forward in a way that is much more reflective of herself—both her humor and her

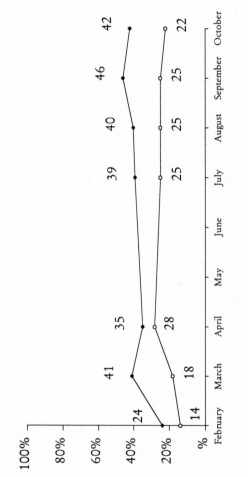

Figure 3.1 Average Favorable and Unfavorable Ratings, Hillary Rodham Clinton, 1992 Campaign

advocacy work for children.... Bill and Hillary need to clarify Hillary's role as First Lady. Ambiguity looks like a power game. It is very important that voters feel comfortable with Hillary's role and not see her as an empowered Nancy Reagan" (Goldman et al. 1994: 663).

But Clinton operatives saw the negative view of Hillary changing by the end of the Democratic convention. In a memo to Bill Clinton, Stan Greenberg reported:

> Hillary Clinton's favorability has risen steadily in this period, paralleling the gains for Bill Clinton. Her mean favorability stood at 41.7 degrees [on a 0-100 "thermometer scale"] before Gore, but rose steadily to 50 degrees and a net positive by Wednesday night. Moreover, there was an utterly new reaction to Hillary in the dial groups. In June, the mean line usually dropped down when Hillary appeared on the screen, but at the convention Thursday night that all changed: the line held steady or moved up (Goldman et al. 1994: 702).

Group Support and Opposition

That she would be more popular with some groups of people than others and that the media would highlight these differences emerged early in the campaign. For example, the *USA TODAY* headline regarding its March poll read "Women, Young Rate Hillary Clinton Highest" (Castaneda and O'Donnell 1992). Original data are available from two sets of national 1992 campaign surveys which provide the opportunity to examine in more detail the polarizing nature of Hillary Rodham Clinton in that election. I use these data to explore who her supporters and detractors were and to gain a perspective of the cultural bases of her support. The data sets are the American National Election Study conducted by the University of Michigan and two CBS polls.

For the first time in their series of election studies, the 1992 American National Election Study included the potential First Ladies in their "feeling thermometer" questions about political leaders and other people in the news.[10] How warmly did people feel about Hillary Clinton? Nine percent of survey respondents said they could not rate Hillary Clinton on the feeling thermometer scale because they did not know enough about her or did not recognize her name. Twenty-six percent rated her at 50 degrees, feeling neither warm not cold, while 43 percent felt warm toward her (rating their feelings above 50 degrees on the scale) and 23 percent felt cold (rating her below 50 degrees).[11] Her mean thermometer rating was 55 degrees. Bill Clinton's was 56 degrees. Respondents tended to feel both colder (30 percent) and warmer (56 percent) toward the candidate than his wife. More were indifferent to Hillary (rating her at 50 degrees) than Bill (14 percent).

Two July and August CBS/NYT polls are pooled together for analysis purposes.[12] These polls asked respondents "Is your opinion of Hillary Clinton favorable, not favorable, undecided, or haven't you heard enough about Hillary Clinton yet to have an opinion?" In these polls, over one-half of the respondents were either undecided or had not heard enough to form a judgment, 33 percent were favorable, and 16 percent were unfavorable.

Men and women did not diverge in their response to the future First Lady at this point. Women expressed only a slightly greater degree of warmth than men in the ANES study. The average feeling thermometer score was 56 degrees for women and 53 degrees for men. The CBS polls also showed no sex differences in attitudes at this stage. Thirty-three percent of women and 32 percent of men were favorable. In post-1994 election analyses, "angry white males" were seen as dominating that election. Hillary Rodham Clinton was viewed as a target of their anger. But during the 1992 election it was not disproportionately white men who expressed the most intense dislike for her. To test the hypothesis of greater intense antiparty on the part of white men, respondents in the ANES study were divided into two groups: those who rated Hillary Clinton on the thermometer at 20 degrees or lower and those who rated her above 20 degrees. Ten percent of white men and nine percent of everyone else rated her at the "frigid" end of the scale.

Blacks were substantially more positive than whites on the ANES thermometer. Blacks had an average score of 62 degrees, while whites had a score of 54 degrees. Thirty-five percent of blacks and 33 percent of whites were favorable towards Hillary Clinton in the CBS polls. Whites were more likely to be unfavorable and less likely to be undecided than blacks. Sixteen percent of whites compared with 6 percent of blacks said they were unfavorable, while 59 percent of blacks and 51 percent of whites were undecided.

Age, education, and income had little impact on feeling thermometer scores for the future First Lady. In the CBS polls, 40- to 49-year-olds were above the average in their favorable opinions—40 percent compared with the overall average of 33 percent. They were less likely to be undecided and as likely to be unfavorable as other age groups. But other age groups did not deviate from the overall average. People with different amounts of formal education and different levels of income tended to rate her similarly.

Not unexpectedly, party affiliation was strongly related to feelings toward Hillary Clinton. Democrats had an average thermometer score of 65, Republicans had an average score of 43, and independents tended to rate her at 54 degrees. In statistical terms, the correlation between ratings on the ANES thermometer and strength of party identification was .47, (p = .001), a quite strong relationship. Party affiliation was also the major factor dividing positive from negative opinions in the CBS polls. Democrats, Republicans, and independents were equally likely to be undecided—51 percent of each group. But 41 percent of self-identified Democrats compared with 34 percent of independents and only 24 percent of Republicans responded in these surveys that they were favorably disposed toward the would-be First Lady. Nearly one-quarter of the Republicans said they were unfavorable (24 percent); only 8 percent of the Democrats felt this way and 15 percent of independents felt this way.

Table 3.1 presents the coefficients from a multivariate analysis of the CBS and ANES data to test more precisely the relationship between these sociodemographic factors and impressions of Hillary Clinton. In multivariate analysis, we examine how a set of variables jointly affect another variable, in this case the effect of sociodemographic factors—age, education, race, income, sex, and party affiliation—on the public's attitude toward Hillary Clinton during the 1992 campaign. Support, for example, may be a function of both one's age and education. In multivariate analysis, we can examine the impact of one variable taking into account (or controlling for) the effect of other variables. The coefficients presented show the relative strength of each relationship controlling for all of the others.

In the multivariate analysis of the ANES data, these variables (age, education, income, sex, race, and strength of party identification) explained 21 percent of the variance in feelings toward Hillary Clinton, with only the party strength variable proving significant (Table 3.1).[13] The multivariate analysis of the CBS polls in Table 3.1 examines supporters and nonsupporters. Undecideds are excluded. The CBS model is estimated using logit regression because of the dichotomous dependent variable. As with the ANES data, analysis of the CBS poll data found only party affiliation having a statistically significant effect on attitudes toward Hillary Clinton. Democrats were her strong supporters while Republicans, not surprisingly, were her detractors. But men and women seemed not to be viewing her in very different lights, nor was there a clash among age groups or classes. The coefficient for sex is negative, indicating men were slightly more favorable than women at this time, controlling for all the other factors (and with undecideds excluded).

In a separate logistic regression analysis of the CBS polls examining the difference between undecideds and those expressing an opinion (regardless of whether it was negative or positive), undecideds were more likely to be younger persons with less education and less income. No statistically significant difference existed between the sexes. Republicans were not more undecided than others, nor were Democrats more opinionated.

Table 3.1
Multivariate Analysis of Group
Support for Hillary Clinton

Factor	ANES survey	CBS Poll
Sex	.006	-.07
Age	.02	-.01
Income	-.02	.04
Education	.00	.04
Race	.01	.47
Party Strength	.45	NA
Democrat	NA	1.01**
Republican	NA	-.79**
Adjusted R^2 =	.21	

ANES = standardized regression coefficients; CBS = logit regression coefficients. Race was coded 0=white, 1=black; sex was coded 0=male, 1=female; party strength went from 1=strong Democrat to 7=strong Republican.
**p = .001

To summarize, during the campaign for the presidency in 1992, these data show that Hillary Clinton was viewed primarily as a partisan figure. Cultural differences that we might have expected to be reflected in age, education, and sex differences in support did not appear.

In addition to the effects of partisan factors, we should expect that political attitudes would separate supporters from opponents of this potential First Lady and that, especially, proponents of women's rights would be among Hillary's advocates while proponents of traditional values would be much less supportive. Sapiro and Conover (1993) have tested the impact of these factors on affect for Hillary Clinton. Using the ANES data, Sapiro and Conover developed a much more inclusive model than that presented in Table 3.1—19 variables in all—including a number of economic perspectives, values, and issue positions as well as demographic and partisan factors to explain variation in thermometer scores for Hillary Clinton. In their model, variance explained increased to 31 percent with partisanship and affect toward her spouse by far the most substantial contributors to that variance. The Hill-Thomas hearings and the issues of abortion and moralism also produced statistically significant differences among respondents in their feelings toward Hillary Clinton.

In the end, what effect did Hillary Rodham Clinton have on the election of 1992? How large a role did she play in the campaign as whole? Did she have an impact on voters? To address the first question, we can peruse the literature on the campaign. In their analysis of the election, political scientist Gerald Pomper and his colleagues in *The Election of 1992* barely mention Hillary Rodham Clinton. She is not referenced in the index, and her visibility that created much media attention is not examined. However, in *Democracy's Feast: Elections in America*, edited by political scientist Herbert Weisberg, which analyzes the 1992 election from a scholarly perspective, a chapter is devoted to "The Candidates' Wives" (Mughan and Burden (1995). The chapter analyzes the "thermometer score" data from the ANES study used in this work. I have noted earlier that the wives of the candidates were included for the first time because of Hillary Clinton's challenge to traditional gender roles. Thus, her presence was the initial catalyst that made "The Candidates Wives" a component of *Democracy's Feast.*

Turning to the work of journalists, we find that Jack Germond and Jules Witcover's *Mad as Hell* (1993), a chronology and analysis of the election as a whole does not have her playing a defining role. This work only peripherally mentions her problems and influence. But she was clearly a major presence in the development of Clinton campaign strategy as reflected in the overview of the campaign by Goldman et al. in *Quest for the Presidency: 1992* (1994). These authors had access to the daily operations of the Clinton effort, and Hillary's presence loomed large from that angle. Further, as shown earlier, she was the subject of media stories to a much greater extent than other candidates' wives, even to receiving prime coverage in national news magazines and being interviewed by the editorial staff of one of the major national newspapers. We must conclude that her centrality to the history of the election was somewhat unprecedented but variable as observed from the lens of expert campaign observers—both academic and journalistic.

Her effect on the voters was also noted in the campaign. In April, interestingly at a point when Hillary appeared to be a campaign liability rather than an asset, "the Gallup Organization calculated the Hillary Factor in a race between Clinton and Bush. Making an admittedly 'rough' analysis, Gallup Vice President Larry Hugick said the Hillary effect actually meant a gain for her husband of 1.6 percent" (Corcoran 1993). Mughan and Burden (1995), in their analysis of the influence of the candidates' wives on votes for their husbands in 1992 using the ANES data I have used above, concluded that Hillary Rodham Clinton was an electoral asset to her husband. The results of a multivariate analysis showed that affect for Hillary had a statistically significant positive effect on the vote for Bill Clinton, these authors reported. Thus, in the end, rather than being a drag on the ticket, she seemed to help her husband, at least as indicated by this piece of statistical data.

The campaign certainly posed problems in reconciling the role of First Lady, or that of the spouse of President, with greater equality and individual achievement for women. The people's response to Hillary Clinton and the discussion and debate about private and public roles were distinctive phenomena of the campaign. There is no doubt that she rates high in the folklore of the 1992 election. She forced attention on women's roles in American society in new ways. I turn now to an examination of what happened to people's perspectives once she entered the White House and began transforming the First Ladyship. These changes will have the most lasting impact on what women can be and how they can achieve in the political realm.

Notes

1. The candidate's words may have been a calculated effort to attract the more liberal primary votes of the Democratic Party.

2. Since some articles from the latter two sources are included in the Proquest compilation, duplication exists, and the reader should not just add together the results of this survey.

3. This is the way her name was referenced in the newspaper index.

4. In 1988, the *New York Times* indexed 29 stories about Kitty Dukakis, wife of the Democratic nominee, Michael Dukakis, seven of which were about her health problems. Barbara Bush rated six references in that year's index.

5. This group does not present any data regarding the distribution of male and female reporters covering the election. It may be that female reporters were disproportionately getting bylines on Hillary Clinton relative to their presence.

6. The percentages on her personal characteristics are given in Chapter 6.

7. What they don't tell readers is the percentage of respondents who thought Hillary would make a poor First Lady and how many said "don't know" to the question. Just comparing the favorable responses at this early stage of introducing Hillary Rodham Clinton to the public does not tell the whole story.

8. The polls included were Gallup, Yankelovich, the *Washington Post*/ABC, CBS/NYT, NBC/WSJ, and *Newsweek*. The average in different months varies in part because the different pollsters used different questions. Question wording has an effect of the distribution of responses. A discussion of this effect is presented in the next chapter.

9. The dial technique involves assembling a group of people in a room, showing them a video presentation of ads and speeches, and asking them to register their responses by turning a dial on a handheld electronic meter (Goldman et al. 1994: 255).

10. Interviewees are told that "ratings between 50 degrees and 100 degrees mean that you feel favorable and warm toward the person. Ratings between 0 degrees and 50 degrees mean that you don't feel favorable toward the person and that you don't care too much for that person. You would rate the person at the 50 degree mark if you don't feel particularly warm or cold toward the person. If we come to a person whose name you don't recognize, you don't need to rate that person." The inclusion of Hillary Clinton and Barbara Bush in the feeling thermometers resulted from interest in gender

and feminism issues among ANES officials which led to the inclusion of a question on Hillary. For balance Barbara Bush was then included according to Virginia Sapiro of the Board of Directors of ANES.

11. The remainder of the respondents in the survey said they were not able to rate her.

12. The percentages do not add to 100 percent because of rounding.

13. Significance here refers to statistical significance which indicates how confident we are that if we could measure the opinions of the whole population and not just a sample that a relationship would exist between the variable.

CHAPTER 4

Public Perceptions of the First Lady

General Impression of Hillary Rodham Clinton as First Lady

In anticipation of her taking on the job of First Lady, *U.S. News & World Report* asked the public in January 1993: "What kind of a job do you think Hillary Clinton will do as first lady?" Seventy-two percent thought she would do either an excellent (30 percent) or a good (42 percent) job, while 18 percent felt she would do only a fair job and 5 percent thought poor (Walsh 1993). In the first two years of the Clinton administration, the public has frequently been asked if it had a favorable or unfavorable opinion of Hillary (or Hillary Rodham) Clinton. National polls have made people's impressions of Hillary as First Lady a major inquiry. Four polls have most consistently explored public opinion of Hillary Clinton: Yankelovich/*Time*/CNN, NBC/WSJ, Gallup/*USA TODAY*/CNN, and CBS/NYT. In the first two years of the administration, they polled on how she was doing on almost a monthly basis just as they polled on the President. As shown in Chapter 3, Hillary Rodham Clinton was a popular subject of poll inquiries from the beginning of the 1992 campaign. In this chapter, I focus on the level of her popularity as First Lady and the approval of the job she has been doing in that role in the first two years of the administration.

Here are the questions as presented by these four polls.

Yankelovich/*Time*/CNN:
Please tell me whether you have generally favorable or generally unfavorable impressions of that person, or whether you are not familiar enough with that person to say one way or the other.

NBC/WSJ:
I'm going to read you the names of several people and institutions who are active in public affairs. I'd like you to rate your feelings toward each one as either very positive, somewhat positive, neutral, somewhat negative, or very negative. If you don't know the name, please just say so.

Gallup/*USA TODAY*/CNN:
I'd like your overall opinion of some people in the news. In general, do you have a favorable or unfavorable opinion of...?

CBS/NYT:
Is your opinion of Hillary Clinton favorable, not favorable, undecided, or haven't you heard enough about Hillary Clinton yet to have an opinion?

Between January 1993 and December 1994, these four national polls assessed Hillary Clinton's favorability with the public a total of 63 times. Figures 4.1 through 4.4 trace the results of these four polls during the first two years of the Clinton administration. (In addition, the *Washington Post*, *U.S. News and World Report*, the *Los Angeles Times*, *Newsweek*, and The Times Mirror Center conducted national polls on her favorability or job approval during this time.)

The Effect of Question Wording. The extent of the First Lady's popularity at a particular time varied depending on the poll. Poll differences on the First Lady's popularity as shown in these four figures illustrate one of the basic issues in polling: the effect of question wording. Whereas Gallup, Yankelovich, and CBS ask about favorable and unfavorable opinions, NBC asks respondents to rate their feelings toward a person as either very positive, somewhat positive, neutral, somewhat negative, or very negative. When given only one positive and one negative option as in the three former polls, people are more likely to go with the positive option; however, a rating scale allows people to spread themselves out in the middle ranges and into less positive ratings without being totally negative.[1]

A second methodological issue also becomes evident as one looks across these opinion ratings. Since January 1993, CBS/NYT has

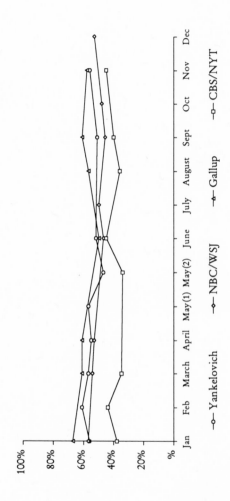

Figure 4.1 Favorability Ratings for Hillary Rodham Clinton 1993

—○— Yankelovich —◇— NBC/WSJ —▲— Gallup —□— CBS/NYT

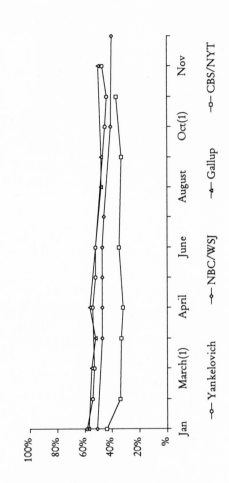

Figure 4.2 Trend in Favorability Ratings for Hillary Rodham Clinton 1994

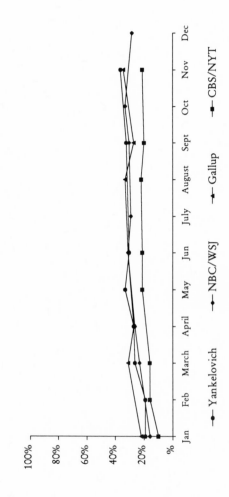

Figure 4.3 Unfavorability Ratings for Hillary Rodham Clinton 1993

Figure 4.4 Unfavorability Ratings for Hillary Rodham Clinton 1994

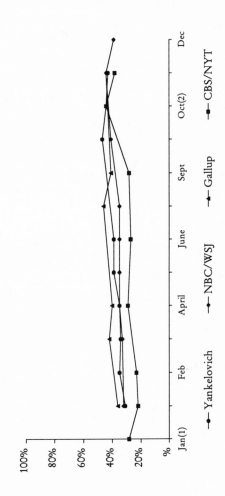

consistently had a smaller portion of respondents making a judgement. This national poll differs from Yankelovich and Gallup by inviting survey participants to say they are undecided in the question. It is not just a volunteered response. "Experimental research shows that many more people will say "don't know' when that alternative is explicitly offered than when it is not" (Converse and Presser 1986, 35). That research is borne out in these polls. The effect of asking different questions is illustrated by a quote from Katha Pollit (1992):

> A Yankelovich survey conducted at the end of March ['92] found that 41 percent of those questioned rated Hillary Clinton favorably, 24 percent unfavorably. *Newsweek*, on the other hand, found that 61 percent liked her and only 16 percent did not. A month later, *U.S. News & World Report* found the country nearly evenly divided--38 percent felt Hillary Clinton helped her husband's campaign while 30 percent felt she hurt it.
>
> Similar confusion reigns when pollsters ask about separate careers for First Ladies. No problem, said a whopping 84 percent in the Yankelovich survey. But according to *USA TODAY*, 67 percent did not want that career to be in her husband's administration. Compare that, though, with *U.S. News & World Report* findings that 66 percent favored Hillary Clinton continuing to work as a lawyer, versus 58 percent who wanted her to be a "traditional First Lady"—numbers that, you may have noticed, don't add up.

The questions are not the same either.

Thus, we get a very different picture of Hillary Rodham Clinton's popularity in the first year of the Clinton administration depending upon whether we use Gallup's poll or we use the CBS/NYT polls. In January at the time of the inauguration, Hillary Rodham Clinton was at the height of her popularity according to Gallup with a 67 percent favorability rating, whereas CBS/NYT reports only a 38 percent favorability because of the much higher percentage of "don't knows" in the latter poll. To control for these discrepancies, Figures 4.5 and 4.6 present an average of her favorable and unfavorable ratings for the first and second years of the Clinton administration. Included in these figures are all of the national polls available in any month, not just the four polls featured in the first

Figure 4.5 Average Favorability/Unfavorability Ratings
for Hillary Rodham Clinton 1993

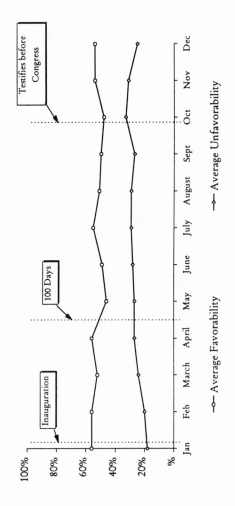

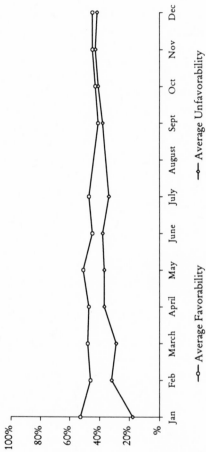

Figure 4.6 Average Favorability/Unfavorability Ratings for Hillary Rodham Clinton 1994

four figures. The inclusion of a larger set of polls wherever available allows us to smooth out monthly blips caused by not all pollsters polling.

The First Year. Hillary Rodham Clinton's favorability ratings peaked as the Clintons entered the White House in January 1993 with 67 percent of the public having a favorable impression in the Gallup Poll.[2] Her support declined somewhat by the 100 days mark but increased again by the end of September at the time of her testimony on the Clinton health care plan before Senate and House committees. Sixty-one percent expressed a favorable opinion in the Gallup Poll at that time. Based on average ratings throughout the year, we can say that she won favorable ratings from over one-half of the public in the first few months of the administration and sustained a positive response from approximately one-half of the people throughout the rest of the year. Her unfavorable ratings inched up over the course of the year from less than 20 percent to approximately three in ten people. The *Redbook* quote that follows illustrates the change from the election to the White House in Hillary Rodham Clinton's popularity.

> These days, though, nobody has a bad word to say about Hillary Clinton. Call it a honeymoon period (her postelection approval ratings have soared), call it collective amnesia, but for the moment, the First Lady can do no wrong. Which is a starkly different picture from last year, when she could do nothing right (Roberts 1993).

At the end of 1993, in their news release reporting results of their December poll, the Times Mirror Center for the People and the Press declared "Hillary's a Hit." "Positive reviews of Hillary Clinton's job performance run well ahead of evaluations made of the President," the release stated (December 9, 1993). She received a 62 percent approval rating for her handling of her duties as First Lady, while 48 percent approved of the job the President was doing. *Vogue* also weighed in noting her triumph:

> This, after all, is Hillary Clinton's moment.... She has... captivated Capitol Hill, and she may well guide her husband through his first real legislative victory. Her numbers in the polls are much higher than his; when he unveiled the health-care plan in front of Congress and the nation, it was she,

seated in the audience between Tipper Gore and new best friend C. Everett Koop, who got two standing ovations. Her testimony to the House committees on Energy and Commerce and Ways and Means turned into a lovefest that ended in applause.... "This is as big as it comes," an aide said before she went on. "This is Eleanor Roosevelt time" (Reed 1993).

Comparison of Bill and Hillary's Ratings. An assessment across polls over time actually shows the President's and First Lady's ratings tracking closely. Figure 4.7 compares favorability ratings of the President and the First Lady based on an average of Yankelovich, NBC, and Gallup polls.[3] She slightly surpassed him in the middle of the first year but fell behind as Whitewater took center stage in media reports in 1994. The close parallel between the ratings of the two indicates the degree to which Hillary Rodham Clinton has been viewed in partisan terms as opposed to a traditional First Lady above the political fray.

The Second Year. At the close of the first year of the Clinton administration, a time during which she had played a major public policy advisory role but had also worked to promote an image of herself performing the traditional family and hostess role, journalists were describing Hillary Rodham Clinton as the "very popular" First Lady. The story was very different in 1994. The Clintons were hit with major attacks concerning their role in what has come to be called the "Whitewater affair." They were slow to respond and lost momentum on public policy concerns as their attention was diverted to defending themselves on this issue. Thus, in the fall of 1994 the administration's health care bill, which was meant to be a center piece of the first administration, was withdrawn from consideration by Congress, and Hillary Rodham Clinton was seen as being instrumental in its defeat. In the election of 1994, she was often the target of attacks by conservatives, especially talk show hosts who dominated the campaign. As Figure 4.6 shows, her favorability ratings declined to where less than one-half of the public was expressing support and as nearly as large a percentage was expressing disapproval. CBS News in their press release of their November 27-28, 1994 poll captures the change:

> Opinions of the First Lady have changed for the worse in recent months, with Americans now as likely to view her

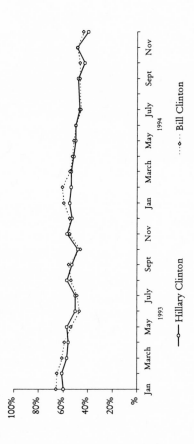

Figure 4.7 Average Favorability Ratings for
Hillary and Bill Clinton 1993-1994

unfavorably as favorably. More than half of the public say Hillary Rodham Clinton should NOT be in a policy-making role. This is a reversal of Americans' reactions when she was first asked to chair the health care reform commission. In fact the public narrowly says her handling of the health care commission was NOT a reason health care reform did not pass last session.

Overall opinion about the First Lady in this poll differs by party and by gender. Republicans are two to one negative; Democrats are as overwhelmingly positive. Women are favorable; men are not. White men seem especially negative towards Hillary Clinton. Only 38 percent of them hold a favorable view of the First Lady, while 59 percent are unfavorable (CBS News Press Release, 11/29/1994).

The reversal in her fortunes is clearly illustrated in the American National Election Study's post-1994 survey in which respondents were asked to rate Hillary Clinton on a thermometer scale as they had in the ANES 1992 survey. Her mean rating had fallen from 55 degrees in 1992 to 48 degrees in 1994. The President's mean score was 54 degrees. The correlation between their scores was .78. (It was .70 in the 1992 survey.) Of those rating the President and First Lady, almost twice as many placed the First Lady at zero degrees (16 percent) as the President (9 percent). Twenty-five percent each placed them at between one and 49 degrees. Nine percent and 13 percent, respectively, placed the President and First Lady at 50 degrees. Fifty-eight percent felt at least somewhat warm toward the President, placing him above 50 degrees, while 46 percent were warm toward the First Lady placing her above 50 degrees. These data suggest she was both a more polarizing and less popular figure in the 1994 election than her husband.

Rather than asking the public about their general impression of the First Lady, pollsters have occasionally inquired as to whether respondents approved or disapproved of the job she was doing as First Lady. Listed below are examples of the results of these inquiries for Hillary.

Harris Poll: How would you rate the job Hillary Rodham Clinton is doing as first lady?*

	June '93	Oct. '93	July '94
Excellent	11%	36%	17%
Pretty good	34	38	39
Only fair	30	17	23
Poor	16	7	18

Gallup Poll: Do you approve or disapprove of the way Hillary Rodham Clinton is handling her job as First Lady?

	Jan. '93	Mar. '94	Apr. '94
Approve	67%	58%	56%
Disapprove	16	39	37
No opinion	17	3	7

U.S. News & World Report, Jan. 1994: Do you approve or disapprove of the way Hillary Rodham Clinton is handling her job as First Lady?

Approve strongly	31%
Approve	26
Disapprove	10
Disapprove strongly	21

Times Mirror, Dec. 1993: Do you approve or disapprove of the way Hillary Clinton is handling her duties as First Lady?

Approve	62%
Disapprove	24

*Figures do not add to 100 percent because "don't knows" and refusals are excluded from the table.

Opinions in the States

Not only has Hillary Rodham Clinton been deemed worthy of national pollsters' attention, interest in the public's reaction to her has been high in the states where both media and academic survey units have polled their citizens about their impressions of her. Through the spring of 1994, polls had been taken in at least 14 states. In the first year, headlines in state newspapers proclaimed her popularity among their citizens. States as diverse as Connecticut, Wisconsin, Virginia, Tennessee, Kentucky, and Ohio reported high favorability ratings.

"Hillary Clinton's Support Booms" headlined the *Tennessee Commercial Appeal* in March 1993—"60% Back Nontraditional Wife; President Gets 52%." (Only one-in-four expressed disapproval.) According to the director of the poll, "I was a little surprised that Tennesseans who are reasonably conservative on a lot of things, were perfectly happy with what Hillary Clinton was doing and gave her higher marks" (Davis 1993). In the fall, the *Knoxville News Sentinel* headlined "President Less Popular Than Wife Statewide, Survey Shows: 61% Approve of Hillary; Husband OK with 48%." (Even 44 percent of conservatives approved of her performance, the paper reported.) Her support had declined markedly, however, by the spring of 1994. The Tennessee Poll found only a 40 percent approval rating at that time.

"First Lady Rates High in Ohio," the *Cincinnati Post* reported in May, 1993, and according to the *Des Moines Register*, "Iowans Give Thumbs Up to First Lady." Her approval rating in Ohio was 61 percent. His approval rating was 47 percent. "Though Hillary Rodham Clinton has drastically redefined the position, most Ohioans approve of the way Mrs. Clinton is handling her job as first lady...." Nineteen percent disapproved of her handling of the role of First Lady. Reasons cited for approving her performance included her work on national health care reform, her general intellectual ability, and educational qualifications (McClung 1993).

Hillary Clinton won approval from 70 percent of Iowans. "In the opening months of her husband's term, Hillary Clinton has emerged as perhaps the most publicly prominent first lady since Eleanor Roosevelt. And so far, Iowans like what they see," the *Des Moines Register* reported (Fogarty 1993).

The same disjuncture between support for the President and the First Lady was reported in Connecticut in May: "President Clinton's popularity in Connecticut continues to sag, but first lady Hillary Rodham Clinton is widely praised and respected for her work," a *Hartford Courant* story ran. The

President received excellent or good marks from 37 percent of those surveyed, while the First Lady was given excellent or good marks by 53 percent. Two-thirds said Hillary Clinton had been a positive influence on the administration, while only 8 percent found her a negative influence.

Table 4.1 summarizes the findings from the various state polls. Examining the polls from the states over time (and keeping in mind that question wording and response options varied across the states), we find a rise over time in her negatives with increasing percentages of respondents saying they either disapproved of the job she was doing as First Lady or had an unfavorable impression of her. Less than a majority in a number of southern state polls viewed her positively in the early months of the administration, but they were not particularly negative in their response relative to other states. They seemed to be more unsure of their feelings.

Table 4.1
Hillary Rodham Clinton's Favorable
Ratings in the States

State	Percent Favorable	Percent Unfavorable
Louisiana—Jan '93	55%	33%
Florida—Feb '93	37	27
Iowa—Feb '93	71	13
Texas—Feb '93	40	27
South Carolina—Feb '93	46	29
Kentucky—Mar '93	40	18
Tennessee—Mar '93	60	26
Texas—Spring '93	57	21

Table 4.1
Hillary Rodham Clinton's Favorable
Ratings in the States, Cont'd

State	Percent Favorable	Percent Unfavorable
Virginia—Mar '93	57	30
California—May '93	50	16
Connecticut—May '93	53	NA
Ohio—May '93	52	17
Iowa—May '93	70	19
Texas—July '93	64	NA
Texas—Summer '93	40	29
Tennessee—Fall '93	61	39
California—Oct '93	50	16
West Virginia—Oct '93	60	35
Wisconsin—Oct/Nov '93	66	30
Montana—Dec '93	52	48
Wisconsin—Dec/Jan	60	33
Connecticut—Jan '94	64	33
Louisiana—Jan '94	55	33
Indiana—Feb '94	56	44
Virginia—Mar '94	50	40
Tennessee—Spring '94	45	40
North Carolina—May '94	46	40

The spring 1994 Southern Focus Poll conducted by the University of North Carolina provides us with a further perspective on regional variations in her popularity. This survey also experimented with the effect of asking respondents about "Hillary Clinton" and "Hillary Rodham Clinton." Table 4.2 shows the findings of this poll. Hillary Rodham Clinton was more popular in nonsouthern regions than Hillary Clinton, but her name made no difference in the South. She was also less popular in the South than in other regions.

Table 4.2
Favorable Ratings for Hillary Clinton
and Hillary Rodham Clinton by Region, Spring 1994

Region	Favorable	Unfavorable	Haven't Heard Enough	Don't Know
South				
HC*	38%	34%	19%	10%
HRC**	36	32	22	11
Nonsouth				
HC*	40	27	25	9
HRC**	47	25	20	8

Southern Focus Poll, March 1994
*Hillary Clinton
**Hillary Rodham Clinton

Group Support and Opposition to the First Lady

Given the dramatic change Hillary Rodham Clinton has made in our perceptions of the role of First Lady, one would expect cultural divisions in evaluations of her and what she stands for regarding women in political leadership. We have found a good deal of variation in people's evaluations of her and her actions as reported in these polls. Substantial numbers of the public have felt warm toward her, and a significant minority have not. In addition, levels of support have changed over time. In this section, I examine levels of support among groups of Americans over time to better understand the cultural basis of support and opposition to her.

Some First Ladies have been viewed as above politics with partisanship having had little effect on their support. People in general felt warm toward them. The public had no reason to substantially oppose them unless they were to project their opinions of her husband, the President, on to the First Lady. However, we should expect differences between those who identify themselves as Democrats and those who identify themselves as Republicans in their views of Hillary, given her partisan nature and involvement in public policy. But how sharp those differences have been and the nature of political independents' assessment should be empirically tested. We would also hypothesize that women would express more positive feelings than men, especially younger women and women in the work force, and that baby-boomers would give her the highest ratings. They would identify with her. Hillary was often the target of conservative talk radio during the 1994 campaign and viewed as a target of disapprobation by "white males" in the aftermath of that election. In this section, I examine the degree to which this presumed cultural divide emerged in national polls.

That Hillary Rodham Clinton would not be viewed as a nonpartisan First Lady admired by the vast majority of Americans was apparent early on as the Clintons made their run for the White House. Journalists quickly noted that she was supported more by some groups than others. *USA TODAY* headlined in March 1992 that she rated highest among women and the young. However, by November 1992, that same newspaper noted that "Women and *older* people have the most favorable opinion of Hillary Clinton." (Emphasis is this author's.) Among women most likely to identify with the First Lady designate were easterners, college graduates, and urbanites, *USA TODAY* reported. Those least likely to identify with her were Midwesterners, suburbanites, high school dropouts, and baby boomers. However, nearly a year later according to the same newspaper, the First Lady was back to being most popular among the young (Benedetto 1993).

Age, Education, Income, and Race. An analysis of the relationship between age and impressions of Hillary Rodham Clinton in 12 surveys conducted throughout 1993 and 1994 reveals little relationship between age and support for her. In these polls, I divided respondents into four age groups—those under 30, those between either 30 and 44 or between 30 and 49 depending on the structure of the data made available, those between 45 and 59 or 50 and 64, and those beyond these age groups. In most of the data sets, no significant differences separated the age groups. The only relationship that emerged at all, and when it emerged it was consistent, was that the oldest age group was more supportive than any other age group. But this was an infrequent occurrence. When it emerged, the characteristic of the relationship was not necessarily one of a monotonic increase; that is, a substantial difference in levels of support may have existed between the youngest aged group and the oldest, but support did not increase incrementally from young to older age respondents. Baby-boomers were not her most loyal supporters. If any age group was, it was older citizens. This is probably because they tended to be the most loyal to the Democratic Party because they were the most liberated group of citizens.

Education and income also seemed to have little effect on one's support for Hillary Rodham Clinton. Most often those with the highest levels of education, i.e., a bachelor's or post-graduate degree were substantially more supportive than those with less than a high school education. Income was quite variable as a predictor of support. In some surveys those with the highest levels of income were much more supportive than those with the lowest levels of income, and in other cases the relationship was reversed. Race did matter, with blacks consistently more supportive than whites.

Sex and Support.   Women have consistently been more favorably disposed toward Hillary Rodham Clinton than men, but at the time the Clintons entered the White House, the differences were small (Figure 4.8). The gender gap grew in the spring of the first year as women's support remained strong and men's started to wan. Men's support began to bounce back in the fall of 1993 and then plunged in the early months of 1994 as Whitewater became prominent in the news. Women's support declined very little after a decrease in the summer of 1993.

In January 1993, 69 percent of women and 65 percent of men approved the way Hillary Clinton was handling her job as First Lady according to Gallup, for example. In April, 67 percent of women and 54 percent of men had a favorable opinion; in June 60 percent of women but only 40 percent of men said they had a favorable opinion of her—a 9-point drop for women but a 25 point decline among men during this six-month period. An especially large gap had emerged in the early months of 1994 as women maintained a quite high level of support while less than half of the men were supportive. Men by this time were as likely to have an unfavorable impression as a favorable one, while women were twice as likely to be

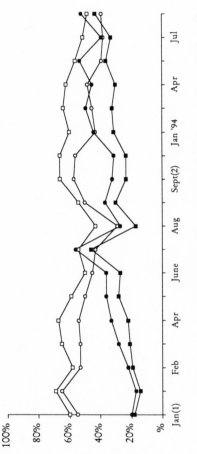

Figure 4.8 Favorability Ratings for Hillary Rodham Clinton by Sex

—○— Men - Favorable   —□— Women - Favorable   —●— Men - Unfavorable   —■— Women - Unfavorable

favorably impressed as unfavorably impressed. In April of 1994, the Harris Poll asked about the job Hillary Rodham Clinton was doing as First Lady. Among women, 53 percent said she was doing an excellent or pretty good job while, 43 percent gave her only a fair or poor rating. The figures were nearly the reverse for men; 52 percent gave her only a fair or poor rating, and 45 percent said she was doing an excellent or pretty good job.

Partisanship and Support.   In January 1993, Gallup reported 53 percent of Republicans and 81 percent of Democrats approving of Hillary Clinton's handling of the job of First Lady, while 64 percent of independents gave her positive marks. By April, Republican support had dropped to 39 percent while Democrats maintained an 83 percent favorable rating, and independent impressions had dropped slightly to 58 percent, according to the Gallup Poll. As the administration proceeded, Democrats remained steadfast in their support while usually less than one-third of Republicans gave her favorable marks. The support of independents, always between that of Democrats and Republicans, declined overtime in the first months of the administration, bounced back and then drifted downward, so that whereas over 60 percent of the independents rated her favorably at the beginning of the administration, their support declined to 50 percent in the second year (Figures 4.9a and 4.9b).

Sex, Partisanship, and Support.   The interaction between sex and party in impressions of the First Lady are intriguing (Figure 4.10). For example, in the June 1993 Gallup Poll only 23 percent of Republican men and 39 percent of Republican women had a favorable opinion of the First Lady compared with 60 percent of Democratic men and 75 percent of Democratic women. A large gap also existed between the support of independent men and independent women. Only 35 percent of the former, but 60 percent of the latter, had a favorable opinion in that poll. Early in the administration, the First Lady seemed to be advantaged by the support she received from independent women and her disproportionate support from Republican women relative to Republican men. The gender gap among Republicans was sustained in the second year of the administration. In April 1994, Gallup attributed the continued gender gap in favorability ratings of Hillary Rodham Clinton "mostly to a gender gap among Republicans: 46 percent of GOP females, compared with 24 percent of GOP males, have a favorable view of

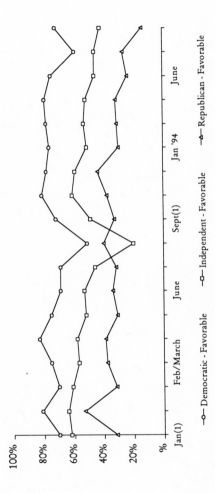

Figure 4.9a Favorability Ratings for Hillary Rodham Clinton by Party

—o— Democratic - Favorable   —□— Independent - Favorable   —▵— Republican - Favorable

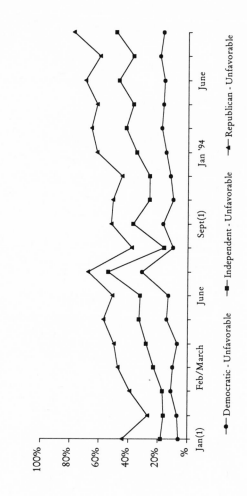

Figure 4.9b Unfavorability Ratings for Hillary Rodham Clinton by Party

Figure 4.10 Favorability Ratings for Hillary Rodham Clinton by Sex and Party

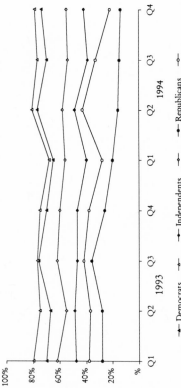

Hillary Clinton, a gap of 22 points. Among Democrats, however, there is only a six point gap: 82 percent of females and 76 percent of males are favorable toward the First Lady." These figures suggest a sharp gender gap in support for Hillary Clinton with women considerably more supportive than men, regardless of party identification.

Multivariate Analyses of Support. How statistically significant are the various sociodemographic relationships described above in assessing support for the First Lady? I have primarily discussed support among each group separately to this point but have not shown how strong or weak the relationships have been statistically. A statistical analysis of the individual relationships would not be comprehensive because groups can be overlapping. For example, blacks tend to identify with the Democratic Party. Thus, if one finds that blacks and Democrats tend to be favorable toward Hillary Rodham Clinton, we are talking to a degree about the same people. Multivariate statistical techniques aid us in sorting out this problem by allowing one to incorporate multiple variables into the model all at once instead of one at a time, and they tell us the extent to which variation in support is accounted for by these characteristics of respondents in a survey.

Table 4.3 presents the results of multivariate analyses of the relationship of the characteristics discussed above to favorability ratings of Hillary Rodham Clinton in the polls for which original data have been made available. The multivariate analyses statistically confirm that Hillary's base of support has been largely among Democrats and women. Party is consistently the major predictor of impressions of her, with Democrats strongly positively impressed and Republicans nearly equally as opposed. Sex, too, has a large effect, with women also consistently more supportive than men. Income, age, and education as shown in the figures do not meaningfully distinguish between supporters and nonsupporters. Support is positively but weakly related to education, while the relationship of age and income varies across polls, showing no pattern of support. Blacks are consistently more supportive than whites, and even when party identification is controlled for, the relationship tends to remain statistically significant.

Table 4.3 Multivariate Analyses of Group Support of Hillary Rodham Clinton, by Quarters of the Year, 1993-1994[4]

	1st Quarter 1993 ABC Ja93	*Time* F/M 93	2nd Quarter 1993 *Time*	3rd Quarter 1993 *Time*	4th Quarter 1993 Times Mirror 12/93
Sex	.52c	.46[b]	.34[c]	.21	.52[b]
Race	.05	.79[a]	.65[c]	.40	.95[a]
Income	.04	-.08	-.02	-.08	-.05
Age	-.00	-.05	.02	-.01	-.003
Education	.10	.08	-.03	.14	.03
Party ID	.67[c]	---	---	---	.40[c]
Democrat	---	.84[c]	1.05[c]	1.05[c]	---
Republican	---	-1.22[c]	-.96[c]	-.61[a]	---

Adjusted R_2

	1st Quarter 1994 US News 1/94	South 3/94	2nd Quarter 1994 Harris 4/94	3rd Quarter 1994 US News 7/94	4th Quarter 1994 US News 10/94
Sex	.16[c]	.19	.09[a]	.16[c]	.13[c]
Race	.06	1.71[a]	.04	.09[a]	.05
Income	---	-.04	-.05	-.07	---
Age	.08	.00	-.01	.06	.03
Education	.09[a]	.19[a]	.08[a]	.08	.08[a]
Party ID	---	.54[c]	.40[c]	.38[c]	.53[3]
Democrat	.92[c]	---	.23[c]	NA	NA
Republican	-.82[c]	---	-.22[c]	NA	NA
Adjusted R_2	.23		.18	.21	

a = p>.01   b = p>.001   c = p>.0001

The figures in the columns are coefficients. They can run from -1 to
0 to +1. The closer to -1 or to +1 they are, the stronger the
relationship. The closer to 0, the weaker the relationship. Coefficients
in Table 1 are logit coefficients unless otherwise specified by the
inclusion of an adjusted R^2. Those coefficients are standardized
regression coefficients.

A positive coefficient indicates women were more supportive than
men, and nonwhites were more supportive than whites. Party
identification goes from strong Republican to strong Democrat.
Democrat and Republican are dichotomous variables.

Only respondents expressing positive or negative opinions are
included in the multivariate analyses.

**The 1994 American National Election Study and Thermometer Scores
for Bill and Hillary.** In the ANES 1994 post-election survey, feelings
toward Hillary Clinton were more polarized between men and women than
they were for Bill Clinton. Hillary's mean score was 43 degrees for men and
52 degrees among women. Bill's was 52 percent among men and 57 percent
among women. At this time, women felt warmer toward the President than
the First Lady. Partisanship played a slightly stronger role in feelings toward
the President. The correlation was .60, while it was .51 for the First Lady.

In the standard multivariate sociodemographic model, attitudes among
groups had crystallized (Table 4.4). Thirty-four percent of the variance was
explained with strength of party identification remaining the most strongly
related factor regarding feelings of warmth or coldness toward Hillary
Clinton. Sex and race were also significant predictors and education was
positively related. Only age had no effect on feelings toward the First Lady.
Table 4.4 compares the results of the multivariate analyses for the President
and First Lady. As reflected in the bivariate analyses, sex was more strongly
related to attitudes toward Hillary than to Bill. In addition, the sign of the
education variable reverses for the President with those having lower levels
of education more supportive than those with higher levels. This set of
predictors also explains more of the variation in feelings toward the
President than toward the First Lady. Most of the feelings toward Bill Clinton
are driven by partisanship whereas the model is more complex for Hillary
Rodham Clinton with more factors having an effect on attitudes toward her.

Table 4.4
Multivariate Analyses of Feeling Thermometer Scores and
Sociodemographic Variables, Post 1994 Election Survey

	Bill Clinton	Hillary Clinton
Party ID	.56[c]	.50[c]
Age	.01	-.01
Sex	.02	.10[c]
Education	-.04	.08[b]
Race	.15c	.16[c]
Income	-.00	.02
Adjusted R^2 =	.41	.34

a = p>.01   b = p>.001   c = p>.0001

Given the attention paid to "angry white men" in the 1994 election who, among other things, seemed to be aiming their wrath at Hillary Rodham Clinton, I compared their rating of her on the feeling thermometer with that of everyone else. The mean rating for white males was 40 degrees compared with 53 degrees for all other demographic groups combined. White males rated Bill Clinton at 49 degrees, and other groups rated him at 58 degrees. So both Clintons received significantly less support from white males, but Hillary, especially, drew their disapproval, giving at least initial empirical support to the media rush to judgment that white men cast their votes against her in that election. Furthermore, 22 percent of white males rated Hillary at zero degrees on the thermometer scale compared with 12 percent of all other groups. Ten percent of white males rated Bill at zero degrees as did 8 percent of all other groups. In 1992, we found no difference in feelings toward Hillary between white males and others as reported in Chapter 3. Although the numbers or respondents are small and less statistically reliable, black women and black men remained highly supportive of the First Lady—the mean score for black men was 69 and the mean score for black women was 75.

Attitudes, Issue Positions, and Support. Beyond sociodemographic correlates, we should expect that the base of Hillary Clinton's support would have been among supporters of the women's rights movement and those in favor of equal rights for women, while those advocating more conservative moral values would be less enthusiastic about her active role as First Lady. Issues should have also played a role.

Thermometer scores for the First Lady were quite strongly related to feelings toward the women's movement (r=.47), somewhat negatively related to feelings toward conservatives (r=-.22), slightly related to feelings toward Christian fundamentalists (r=-.08), and very weakly related to feelings toward gays and lesbians (r=.03). The correlation between opinion on abortion rights and feelings toward Hillary was .15 (p>.001) and .18 (p>.001) for Bill.

The Southern Focus Poll conducted in the spring of 1994 and the ANES 1994 post-election study each asked a series of questions covering a range of opinions on social, economic, and cultural issues in addition to sociodemographic items. For the ANES study, I also compare the contextual basis of thermometer responses for Bill Clinton and Hillary Clinton.

At the bivariate level (meaning a relationship between two variables not controlling for other factors) in the Southern Focus Poll, evidence existed that more religious individuals were less favorably disposed toward Hillary Clinton than those with less religious fervor. Forty-six percent of those who never attended religious services were favorable toward the First Lady compared with 33 percent of those who attended religious services more than once a week, and 47 percent of those who disagreed that the Bible was literally true were favorable compared with 37 percent of those who believed it was literally true.

Seventy-three percent disagreed and 25 percent agreed with the statement "Some equality in marriage is a good thing, but by and large, the husband should have the main say-so." Forty-six percent of those who disagreed had a favorable opinion of Hillary Clinton compared with 30 percent of those who agreed. Respondents were very evenly split between those who thought it was morally wrong for a man or a woman to have sexual relations before marriage—47 percent agreed and 44 percent disagreed.[5] Thirty-five percent of those who agreed with the statement and 47 percent of those who disagreed were favorable toward Hillary Clinton. Finally, 67 percent agreed with the question "Do you think it is morally wrong for a woman to have sexual relations with another woman?" (or morally wrong for a man to have sexual relations with another man),[6] and 23 percent disagreed. Forty-four percent of those who disagreed and 36 percent of those who agreed had a favorable opinion of Hillary Clinton. Consistently in the bivariate situation, Hillary Clinton received stronger support from those who were less religiously inclined, were more believing in egalitarian marriages and more liberal in their beliefs about sexual relations. Table 4.5 includes a subset of these cultural attitudinal variables in a multivariate analysis with our standard sociodemographic variables to test their relative significance.[7] In the multivariate logit model, partisanship continues as a stronger predictor. To a slightly lesser extent race, education, and views on egalitarian marriages impact on impressions of the First Lady. In this model the sex of the respondent drops out as a significant predictor.

Table 4.5

Multivariate Analyses of Sociodemographic and Attitudinal Variables and Support for Hillary Clinton, Southern Focus Poll, Spring 1994[8]

Partisanship	.53[c]
Age	.01
Sex	.16
Education	.24[b]
Race	1.65[a]
Family income	-.05
Bible literally true	-.35
Premarital sex	.48
Egalitarian marriage	.62[a]

a = p>.01   b =p>.001   c = p>.0001
Support for Hillary was coded 0 for "unfavorable" and 1 for "favorable."

The gay sex variable combines in one variable the responses to the questions about sexual relations between men and sexual relations between women.

From the ANES 1994 post-election study, I have included not only cultural attitudinal variables but issue concerns as well (unavailable in the Southern Focus Poll) and compared responses for the President and the First Lady. In the extended model, partisanship continues to be the major force underlying feelings toward both Bill and Hillary Clinton (Table 4.6). For Bill Clinton, race, the state of the economy, government provision of health insurance, and feelings toward the women's movement are particularly related to expressions of support. The same pattern holds for Hillary with the exception of sex, which is also statistically significantly related to feelings about her. In addition, the standardized coefficient for feelings toward the women's movement is higher for Hillary than for Bill. The other values questions—thermometer ratings for Christian fundamentalists and "adjusting moral values with the times" interestingly are not related to feelings toward either the President or his wife controlling for these other factors. Nor in this model are opinions about abortion related to thermometer ratings.

The bases upon which men and women made their judgments about the President were similar for the most part, with the exception of some issue positions. Feelings about national health insurance were more important in men's feelings toward Bill Clinton than women's; for women, the role of government in the creation of jobs was more significant. For both sexes, however, partisanship, the state of the economy, whether they were black or white, and their feelings about the women's movement were the major factors affecting their support for the President.

Men's opinions toward Hillary were also more strongly driven by their opinion of the government's role in health insurance than were women's. Men and women also differed slightly in the intensity with which their views of the economy and raising taxes affected their thermometer scores for Hillary.

Table 4.6
Multivariate Analyses of Feeling Thermometer Scores and Sociodemographic and Attitudinal Variables, Post 1994 American National Election Survey

	Bill Clinton			Hillary Clinton		
	All	Men	Women	All	Men	Women
Partisanship						
Party ID	.38^c	.35^c	.42^c	.32^c	.30^c	.33^c
Demographics						
Age	.05^a	-.00	.10^b	.04	.02	.05
Sex	.02	NA	NA	.10^c	NA	NA
Education	-.08^b	-.08^a	-.06	.05	.08^a	.03
Race	.13^c	.13^c	.13^c	.13^c	.12^c	.14^c
Economics						
Family Income	-.02	.00	-.03	.01	.02	.00
State of Economy	-.15^c	-.15^c	-.16^c	-.13$_c$	-.10^b	-.16^c
Job/Standard of Living	-.10$_c$	-.05	-.13^c	-.08^b	-.08	-.09^a
R Better/ worse off	-.07^b	-.07^a	-.06	-.04	-.06	.00
Issues						
Abortion	.03	.02	.03	.04	.03	.06
Taxes/deficit	-.05	-.08^a	-.01	-.05	-.08^a	-.03
Health Insurance	-.12^c	-.18^c	-.06	-.09^b	-.13^b	-.05
Values						
Therm- Christian Fund.	-.03	-.03	-.03	-.00	.00	-.02
Therm- Women's Move.	.15^c	.17^c	.14^3	.23^c	.24^c	.22^c
Adjust morals	-.04	-.05	-.04	-.06	-.07	-.06
Adjusted R^2 =	.50	.52	.49	.44	.45	.42

The Popularity of Hillary Rodham Clinton in Historical Perspective

How have the public's perceptions of Hillary Rodham Clinton compared with perceptions of her predecessors? Before making some concluding remarks about the public's impressions of Hillary Rodham Clinton as First Lady, I provide here an historical review of extant national polls on other First Ladies.

"Mrs. Roosevelt More Popular Than President, Survey Finds" ran the headline in the *Washington Post* (Gallup 1939). In what was probably the first national survey of public opinion of a First Lady, the Gallup Poll in 1939 asked a national sample *"Do you approve of the way Mrs. Roosevelt has conducted herself as "First Lady"?* Sixty-seven percent said "yes," and 33 percent responded "no." Eighty-one percent of Democrats, and 43 percent of Republicans approved. Women were more supportive than men—73 percent to 62 percent approval. In the same survey, Franklin Roosevelt received a 58 percent approval rating as President.

After this 1939 inquiry, Gallup did not continue to ask the public about their opinions of the First Lady. Not until Jacqueline Kennedy entered the White House in 1961 do we find another national rating of the First Lady. In a Gallup Poll of June 1961,[9] Jacqueline Kennedy received a favorable impression from 59 percent of the public while 13 percent had an unfavorable impression, 6 percent said they had a mixed impression, and 22 percent had no opinion. These are the only national polls available regarding First Ladies prior to the Nixon administration. In 1969, after she had been in the White House for six months, Gallup asked a national sample "Do you approve or disapprove of the way Mrs. Richard (Pat) Nixon is handling her role as 'First Lady?'" Fifty-four percent of the people said they approved of the job Pat Nixon was doing as First Lady; only 6 percent disapproved, and 40 percent said they had no opinion. Responding to a Harris Poll in 1971, 55 percent said they had a "great deal" of respect for Mrs. Pat Nixon, wife of the President, 34 percent said they respected her somewhat, and 9 percent said not at all. (Two percent said they were not sure.) Given a card with boxes going from the highest position of plus 5 for a person liked very much to the lowest position of minus 5 for a person disliked very much, 28 percent rated Mrs. (Pat) Nixon at +5. Fourteen percent rated her at -1 or lower.

In the same rating scheme in 1976, Betty Ford received a +5 from 13 percent of the population, and -1 or lower by 20 percent of the sample. She was viewed positively by 71 percent of the people while 24 percent had a negative opinion in the only national poll available from the Ford administration.[10]

No early readings are available on the public's impression of Rosalynn Carter.[11] But in 1979 she obtained a 55 percent favorable and 33 percent unfavorable response from the public,[12] and during the 1980 campaign she received a 46 percent favorable, and a 9 percent unfavorable rating, while 37 percent said they did not know enough to respond, and eight percent were undecided.[13]

Nancy Reagan began her sojourn in the White House with a 28 percent favorable rating while 10 percent said they had an unfavorable opinion, 57 percent said they did not know enough about her to have an opinion, and five percent had no opinion, according to a CBS/*New York Times* poll. She became quite popular during her time in the White House, especially after the first year, when she began to respond to the negative press she had received for her gifts, table settings, etc. In November 1981, 51 percent responding to an ABC/*Washington Post* poll said they had a favorable impression of Nancy Reagan; 23 percent were unfavorable, and 26 percent didn't know or had no opinion. Sixty-two percent replied in a Gallup Poll of December 1981, that she "puts too much emphasis on style and elegance during a time of federal budget cuts and economic hardships," while 30 percent said they were "pleased with Nancy Reagan because they feel she has brought more style and elegance to the White House." In the same poll, 61 percent thought she was less sympathetic to the problems of the poor and underprivileged compared to other First Ladies, 16 percent thought she was more sympathetic; 9 percent volunteered "the same," and 14 percent said that they did not know.

Through most of the rest of the Reagan administration, Nancy Reagan was viewed favorably by over 60 percent of the people, and occasionally the polls reached a 70 percent positive rating. But her popularity declined by the end of the Reagan administration with a bare majority expressing approval of the First Lady and about three in ten saying they disapproved.

Bush strategists in the 1988 campaign feared that Barbara Bush would be a detriment primarily because "her white hair and wrinkles tended to remind voters of her husband's age" (Campbell 1993, 3). In an NBC October 1988 poll, 48 percent of likely voters said they had a favorable impression of her; 11 percent had an unfavorable impression, and 41 percent said they were unsure.[14] When she entered the White House in January 1989, 34 percent of the public had a favorable opinion, only 3 percent were unfavorable while the remainder were undecided or had not heard enough to give an opinion.[15] After being in the White House for six months, she received an excellent or pretty good job rating from 66 percent of the public, while 28 percent rated her as doing only a fair or poor job.[16] By the 1992 campaign, Barbara Bush was considered a great asset, obtaining an 85 percent favorable rating in an August 1992 poll, while only 9 percent were unfavorable.[17] Seldom did as many as 20 percent of the people view her unfavorably during the Bush administration.

Barbara Bush's ratings with the public were a poll topic at the beginning of the Bush administration and during the campaign of 1992. But during the administration, she was not a subject of national polls. Presumably because of her noncontroversial nature she was not considered a newsworthy item. There was little to dislike about Barbara Bush or to disagree with in her role as First Lady. The people's views of her were a poll item throughout the 1992 campaign, however. We can assume that these poll questions were a reaction to the Hillary Clinton phenomenon, asked to provide a comparative perspective.

Barbara Bush, based on poll ratings, was the most popular First Lady in recent times while Nancy Reagan became the least popular before Hillary Rodham Clinton's tenure in the White House. In general, First Ladies have tended to be quite popular. The public has been much more likely to be favorably impressed than not with the individuals who have held this position and to approve of the job they were doing in it. Prior to Hillary Rodham Clinton's becoming First Lady, the public's views of the person occupying this position were only sporadically solicited, plus opinions were seldom ascertained in the same way across time making it difficult to make comparisons. National pollsters' interest in the First Ladies as political figures rose and fell depending on their either stepping outside the hostess role or not behaving in a properly modest fashion. Questions asked about Betty Ford because of her outspokenness illustrate this point. They are listed below.

1. Let me read you some statements that have been made about Betty Ford. For each, tell me if you tend to agree or disagree.

   a. She ought to keep more of her opinions to herself and let her husband take stands on the issues.

   Agree 39%   Disagree 52%   Not sure 9%

   b. She is brave and courageous, such as when she had her operation for breast cancer and when she said a prayer for a Jewish Leader who had just had a heart attack.

   Agree 86%   Disagree 5%   Not sure 9%

   c. She has stood up firmly for women's rights, and that is good.

   Agree 73%   Disagree 14%   Not sure 13%

   d. She was wrong to talk about what she would do if her daughter were having an affair.

   Agree 42%   Disagree 48%   Not sure 10%

   e. She is too active in her husband's political campaign and should stay more behind the scenes.
   Agree 23%   Disagree 67%   Not sure 10%

2. Do you tend to agree or disagree with Mrs. Betty Ford when she said... she favors passage of the Equal Rights Amendment on women's rights?

   Agree 70%   Disagree 15%   Not sure 15%

3. Do you tend to agree or disagree with Mrs. Betty Ford when she said... she would not be surprised if her daughter had an affair?

   Agree 60%   Disagree 27%   Not sure 13%

4.   Do you tend to agree or disagree with Mrs. Betty Ford when she said...if her daughter were having an affair, she would want to know if the young man were nice or not?

Agree 64%   Disagree 23%   Not sure 13%

Hillary Rodham Clinton was a frequent subject of pollsters' questions, which have served as a basis for this study, because of her challenge to the traditional role of First Lady. In 1995, as she adopted a softer role, pollsters' inquiries about the public's impressions of her declined in number. The Roper Center's archive of public opinion poll questions lists 91 questions about Hillary in 1992, 265 in 1993, 376 in 1994, but only 62 in 1995.[18]

Conclusion

Popularity is an important element in assessing a President. It is significant, too, for the First Lady. The survey data examined to this point suggest that it is possible to transform the First Ladyship into a public partnership with the President and receive a positive response from the public. This conclusion is based on poll results from 1993 regarding the public's impressions of Hillary Rodham Clinton. But lack of success in policy achievement by a First Lady results in a damaging response to the person in that role who might otherwise have served as a consensual symbol in her spouse's administration. Further, a backlash still attends a woman who steps out of the traditional mold that has been socially constructed for her. This is suggested by the ANES 1994 post-election survey, which found a greater polarization in feelings toward Hillary Clinton than toward Bill Clinton. (Bear in mind that we do not have a pure test of the transformation phenomenon because the Clintons' ethical and possible legal problems over Whitewater were prominent political issues in 1994 and affected impressions of them and probably caused public doubt regarding her policy-making role.)

The finding that Hillary Clinton seemed to be successfully combining a politically active First Ladyship with the performance of the traditional ceremonial roles of the First Lady in the first year of the administration actually has historical precedence based on what we know from public opinion polls. We have seen that the one national scientific poll conducted about Eleanor Roosevelt found her to be quite popular. Betty Ford received strong support among the public when she was outspoken on social issues. Rosalynn Carter won approval by a substantial majority of the people for her trip to South America to consult with heads of state as an emissary for the President. Thus, although the public generally advocate for a more traditional First Lady, they tend to applaud those who adopt a more active role as long as they appear to be performing effectively in it.

Poll results suggest a complex response among Americans to a First Lady who engages in the policy aspects of the public realm. Pollsters have also provided us with information concerning the redefining of the First Ladyship beyond general impressions of Hillary Rodham Clinton in the role. They have sought to measure responses to her specific activities as a Presidential adviser. Responses to these questions give us an opportunity to assess in more detail public reaction to Hillary's specific activities as a presidential adviser. I turn to this task in Chapter 5.

Notes

1. This has been found in some of the presidential ratings between questions asking the public whether they approve or disapprove of the job the president is doing, and those asking the public to rate the job the president is doing as either excellent, good, fair, or poor. The latter set of response options tend to elicit lower ratings for the president.

2. Unfortunately few polls exist which asked the same question about other First Ladies at the same time point. The only comparison that can be made is with a CBS poll of January 12-15, 1989, in which 34 percent said they had a favorable opinion of Barbara Bush while three percent were unfavorable and 63 percent were either undecided or had not heard enough.

3. Most polls assessing the President's relationship with the people ask about their approval of his job performance. In order to more clearly compare Bill and Hillary's ratings I have used the subset of polls that have asked people about their favorable or unfavorable impression of the President. I have excluded CBS because they have only sporadically asked people about their views of the President using a favorable/unfavorable scale. If that poll's tracking of the First Lady had been included, it would have substantially lowered her ratings compared with the President because of the distinctive set of response options CBS gives people.

4. The first quarter time points are from the January 1993, ABC/*Washington Post* poll and a combination of *Time* magazine polls from February, March, and April 1993. The second quarter combines *Time* magazine polls from May and June 1993. The South poll in the 1st quarter of 1994 is the Southern Focus Poll conducted in March. It combines a sample of Southern and nonsouthern respondents.

5. Half of the sample was asked about premarital sex for men and half were asked about premarital sex for women.

6. Half of the sample was asked about sexual relations between women and half were asked about sexual relations between men.

7. I use a subset of the cultural attitudinal variables because of the strong relationship between pairs of these variables.

8. Question wording for Table 4.5:
v930 Some people feel the government in Washington should see to it that every person has a job and a good standard of living. Others think the government should just let each person get ahead on their own. Where would you place yourself on this scale, or haven't you thought much about this? (7-point scale)

v902 Would you say that you (and your family living here) are better off or worse off financially than you were a year ago?

v908 How about the economy in the country as a whole. Would you say that over the past year the nation's economy has gotten better, stayed about the same, or gotten worse?

v1014 There has been some discussion about abortion during recent years. Which one of the opinions on this page best agrees with your view?

.1. By law, abortion should never be permitted.

2. The law should permit abortion only in case of rape, incest or when the woman's life is in danger.

3. The law should permit abortion for reasons other than rape, incest, or danger to the woman's life, but only after the need for the abortion has been clearly established.

4. By law, a woman should always be able to obtain an abortion as a matter of personal choice.

v950 There is much concern about the rapid rise in medical and hospital costs. Some people feel there should be a government insurance plan which would cover all medical and hospital expenses for everyone. Others feel that all medical expenses should be paid by individuals, and through private insurance plans like Blue Cross or other company paid plans. Where would you place yourself on this scale, or haven't you thought much about this?

v1030 The world is always changing and we should adjust our view of moral behavior to those changes. (This was an agree or disagree statement.)

9. The question asked was "What are your impressions of Jacqueline Kennedy?"

10. Poll taken by Harris and Associates, July 1976. However, the people were queried on a number of occasions about Betty Ford's active support for women's rights.

11. However, in a poll conducted by Pat Caddell after Rosalynn Carter was sent by the President to visit heads of state in South America for the administration, 70 percent of Americans rated her trip as excellent or good (Jensen 1990, 770).

12 .Yankelovich, October 1979.

13. CBS/*New York Times*, October 1980.

14. At the same time, 42 percent said they had a favorable opinion of Kitty Dukakis, 11 percent were unfavorable, and 47 percent were unsure.

15. CBS/*New York Times*, 1989.

16. Harris Poll, July 1989.

17. Gallup Poll, August 1992

18. These numbers were generated through the Lexis-Nexis database system.

CHAPTER 5

The First Lady
and Public Policy Making

When the Clintons came into office her polls went up dramatically
when she started to work on health care.
- Rosalynn Carter, interview

Pre-administration

In a February 1992 national poll, Yankelovich and Associates asked
"From what you know of Hillary Clinton, do you think she has what it takes
to be President of the United States, or don't you think so?" At that point, 19
percent of the people responded affirmatively, while 40 percent were
negative and 41 percent were unsure. The important point here is not so
much the poll results but the fact that a major pollster thought to ask such a
question, particularly at that early stage of the election. It shows the
immediate impact Hillary Rodham Clinton had on the national electoral
scene as a public political leader and her emergence as a symbol of the
changes the women's movement had wrought.

Pollsters have not been content to ascertain overall impressions of
Hillary Rodham Clinton and to gauge the extent of the public's approval of
the job she has been doing as First Lady as the previous chapter reviewed.
They also have been concerned with her political and policy-making role in
the White House and as a politician in her own right and have polled the
public many times about those issues. Thus, they have provided us with a
wealth of public opinion data on a number of dimensions of Clinton's role as
First Lady. These polls allow for a fuller analysis of reactions to her in this
position and public acceptance of a broader substantive role for the First
Lady.

Hillary Rodham Clinton had been the President's political and policy adviser during his tenure as governor of Arkansas. Her involvement in that administration had not been of the private "behind-the-scenes" variety often characteristic of political wives, rather she had served as a visible political partner. It would have been out of character for her to adopt any other role as First Lady of the nation. Indeed, given her credentials, political observers have noted that had she not been the wife of the President, she would have qualified as an appointee to a position in another Democratic administration. (See, e.g., Beck 1992; Clift and Miller 1992.) Hillary brought to the White House professional credentials as well as personal traits which provided her with a legitimate claim to be a major presidential adviser.

The role she would play in the administration drew major press curiosity after the election. According to David Broder in a November 1992 *Washington Post* editorial "Of all the transition events since Bill Clinton won the presidency, none has occasioned more comment than the presence of future First Lady Hillary Clinton throughout the president-elect's first meeting with Democratic congressional leaders" (1992). President-elect Clinton was quite forthright about her role. "We just sort of sit down here around the table and talk. She's part of it," the President-elect said in response to questions about her participation in his meetings with key transition advisers and congressional leaders. "She stayed the whole time, talked a lot.... She knew more than we did about some things." At a news conference to announce Cabinet appointments, Clinton noted "She advised me on these decisions, as she has on every other decision I've made in the last 20 years" (Ifill 1992).

During the transition Hillary Rodham Clinton was one of only five people in the room, along with Vice-President Gore, transition chief Warren Christopher, and two aides when the President-elect went over names for top jobs (Clift and Miller 1992). She also participated in the two-day economic conference Clinton held in December prior to the inauguration, although she did not ask questions or make comments.

Whether Hillary would hold some kind of Cabinet status was an item of press speculation. A December 19, 1992, *New York Times* headline ran "Clinton Wants Wife at Cabinet Table" (Ifill 1992), and the *Washington Post* headlined "A Clinton in the Cabinet? Not Officially, but First Lady Will Sit in" (Sherrill 1992). Because of the so-called "Bobby Kennedy" law, she could not be appointed to an official position in the government. The Postal Revenue and Federal Salary Act of 1967 passed in response to President John F. Kennedy's appointment of his brother as Attorney General forbids a public official from appointing, employing, promoting, or advancing a relative in an agency in which he is serving or over which he exercises jurisdiction or control. So although she could not be appointed to a formal paid position, Clinton and his transition team said she would attend Cabinet meetings whenever she wanted (Sherrill 1992).

How did the people feel about her taking on a policy advisory role? To summarize poll results prior to the inauguration, we can say that two-thirds were not worried about Hillary Clinton having too large of a role in the Clinton administration (Gallup, 11/1992) and did not see her as having too large of a role in the transition (Clift and Miller 1992). Based on the results of their December 1992 poll, the *Wall Street Journal* concluded that the prospect of Hillary Clinton being an influential White House adviser was "fine by most Americans. By 63 percent to 24 percent, Americans believe Mrs. Clinton has the knowledge and personal characteristics that qualify her to be an adviser to her husband" (Frisby 1992).

But at the same time, the public was sending other messages about what kind of First Lady they preferred. She can be an adviser but should not be appointed to an official position in her husband's administration or sit in on Cabinet meetings people told pollsters (Walsh 1993). Given an option, the U.S. public preferred that Hillary Clinton be a traditional First Lady, advocate for policies and programs to benefit children and testify before Congress on issues that concern her but not sit in on cabinet meetings or be a major adviser on appointments and policy. The following questions from pre-inauguration polls show how the public felt at the time.

Pre-administration Polls on Hillary as Policy Advisor

1. Gallup 4/92: Do you approve or disapprove of Hillary Clinton having a major post in her husband's administration?

   approve   25%   disapprove   67%   not sure   8%

2. Gallup 7/92: Do you favor or oppose having a First Lady who is involved in the President's policy decisions and the day-to-day operations of the White House staff?

   approve   58%   oppose   35%   not sure   7%

3. Gallup 11/10/92: Which worries you more—that Hillary Clinton won't have a large enough role in the Clinton administration or that she will have too large a role, or does neither worry you very much?

Role not large enough	4%
Too large a role	26%
Neither	67
No opinion	3

4. *Newsweek* 11/20/92: Do you think Hillary Clinton is playing too great a role in the transition process?

Not too great	62%
Too great	25

5. NBC/WSJ 12/15/92: Do you believe that Hillary Clinton has the knowledge and personal characteristics that would qualify her to be an advisor to her husband while he serves as president, or not?

HRC qualified to be advisor	63%
Not qualified	24
Not sure	13

6. Would you favor or oppose the appointment of Hillary Clinton to an official position in the Clinton Administration?

Favor appointment	32%
Oppose appointment	59
Not sure	9

7. Would you like to see Hillary Clinton play an active role in policy-making in the Clinton administration?

Newsweek 12/28/92:	Yes	46%		No	40%
Gallup	1/14/93:	Yes	43%	No	53%

8. *Los Angeles Times*, Jan 93: Do you think Hillary Clinton should sit in on the President's Cabinet meetings, or not?

Should   20%   Should not   68%   Don't know   8%

9. CBS/*New York Times*, Jan 93: Do you approve or disapprove of Hillary Clinton sitting in on Cabinet meetings?

Approve 40%   Disapprove 53%   Don't know 7%

10. *U.S. News & World Report* 1/25/93: Do you favor or oppose these roles for Hillary Clinton?

	Favor	Oppose
Sitting in on Cabinet meetings	37%	58%
Being a traditional first lady	70	21
Being an advocate for policies & programs to benefit children	90	7
Being a major advisor on appointments and policy	34	59
Testifying before Congress on issues that concern her	71	22

Advisor to the President

        "'Of course she's in the loop,' says an administration official. 'She *is* the loop'" (Cooper 1993).

        When Hillary Rodham entered the White House, she inherited an established office in the East Wing of the building. An Office of the First Lady has become part of the organizational structure of the Office of the President.[1] This office as an official part of the President's staff is a contemporary phenomenon, but Anthony (1990) and Caroli (1987) trace its beginnings to the Presidency of Theodore Roosevelt. According to these two historians, the institutionalization of an office for the First Lady within the executive branch was initiated when Edith Roosevelt hired a "social secretary" to handle her official correspondence, the first salaried government employee answering to the First Lady as her boss. The duties handled on this side of the White House focused on the social life of the

Presidency; its staff remained small and was not formally recognized as part of governmental personnel until the more contemporary presidency.

Even Eleanor Roosevelt, for all of her travels and involvement in the public life of the nation, had a staff of only two. "At an annual salary of $35,000 [Malvina Thompson] was the first member of the First Lady's staff to be paid as personal secretary, but when she worked on Eleanor's personal business, she was paid by her. A former employee of Edith Wilson, Edith Benham Helm, first volunteered to help Eleanor as a part-time social secretary, and her role quickly evolved into a full-time job" (Anthony 1990, 458). They were "assisted by various White House staffers who worked on temporary assignments" (Caroli 1987, 198).

Evidence of the First Lady's staff being perceived as a formal part of government personnel did not occur until 1953 during the Eisenhower administration when the *Congressional Directory* "acknowledged for the first time the distaff side of the Executive Office [by] list[ing] Mary McCaffree, 'Acting Secretary to the President's wife'" (Caroli 1987, 218).

Jackie Kennedy dramatically expanded the First Lady's staff until eventually Letitia Baldrige her Social Secretary reported that she had "forty people working under her in what she referred to as the 'First Lady's Secretariat' (Baldrige 1968). Her staff was divided into four sections: press, calligraphy-protocol-social records department, correspondence, and social files. But only Letitia Baldrige's position was listed under the Office of the President in the *Congressional Directory*.

Lady Bird Johnson contributed to the development of the First Lady's office by "appointing a larger and better-trained staff than any seen in the East Wing of the White House." Her press section consisted of six full-time employees, and two staff members dealt only with beautification issues. Caroli notes "expertise became as much a mark of the East Wing as the West Wing" under Lady Bird Johnson's tutelage (1987, 242). Activities within her domain "became an extension of the Presidential office—purposeful activities which were designed to complement and supplement programs, policies, and legislation emanating from the Administration" (Foreman 1971, 101).

Contemporary First Ladies established a staff that includes in addition to responsibility for the social and symbolic duties of the office, press personnel, and policy experts for whatever problem became their "issue." For example, the *Congressional Directory* lists a Director of Projects for the First Lady and a Director of Community Liaison in the Carter administration. Since the Reagan administration, the Office of First Lady has been headed by a Chief of Staff. During the Clinton administration, the position of Chief of Staff to the First Lady has been elevated to the status of Assistant to the President (Tenpas, forthcoming).

In 1978, during the Carter administration, Congress for the first time provided legal authority for the existence of an office to fund the administration of the White House in the White House Personnel Authorization-Employment Act (Public Law 95-570). Prior to passage of this bill, federal law had authorized the President only 14 staff members whereas in actually the White House had grown to a staff of over 300. Though Congress annually had approved appropriations for the larger staff, the money had been challenged on the floor several times for its lack of authorization (*CQ Almanac* 1978, 797). The aim of this law was to rectify this situation. What is important for our purposes is that it included authorization for "Assistance and services...to be provided to the spouse of the President in connection with assistance provided by such spouse to the President in discharge of the President's duties and responsibilities." Prior to enactment of this legislation, funds for the First Lady's staff and travel were appropriated on an as needed basis from the general budget line item for White House management (Rosebush 1987, 32).

Hillary Rodham Clinton's staff has consisted of between 14 and 16 people. The list that follows shows the positions composing the First Lady's staff for Clinton, Barbara Bush, Nancy Reagan, and Rosalynn Carter. The major difference in positions (actual duties and responsibilities are a separate issue) is between the Reagan office with its calligraphers and graphic artists and the Bush and Clinton offices, which did not list such positions.

Office of the First Lady

Rosalynn Carter
>Staff Director for the First Lady
>Administrative Assistant to the Staff Director
>Research Assistant
>Personal Assistant to the First Lady
>Personal Security to the First Lady
>Administrative Assistant to the First Lady
>Press Secretary
>Deputy Press Secretary
>Assistant Press Secretary
>Press Aide
>Director of Projects

Assistant to Projects Director
Assistant Director for Community Liaison
Director of Scheduling
Director of Advance
Assistant to Director of Scheduling
Scheduling and Advance Assistant
Assistant to Director of Advance
Social Secretary
Assistant Social Secretary
Assistant to the Social Secretary
Assistant to Social Secretary
Calligraphers (3)

Nancy Reagan

Deputy Assistant to the President
Administrative Assistant
Personal Assistant to First Lady
Press Secretary
Deputy Press Secretary
Executive Assistant
Social Secretary
Assistant Social Secretary
Executive Assistant
Director, Graphics and Calligraphy
Graphics Assistant
Staff Assistant
Calligrapher (2)
Director, Projects & Correspondence
Executive Assistant
Deputy Director, Projects & Correspondence
Staff Assistant
Director, Scheduling of Advance for the First Lady
Deputy Press Secretary for Communications
Secretary
Assistant Chief, Arrangements

Barbara Bush

Deputy Assistant to the President and Chief of Staff to the First Lady
Staff Assistant to the Chief of Staff

Press Secretary
Deputy Press Secretary (2)
Social Secretary
Deputy Social Secretary
Director of Projects
Director of Scheduling
Director of Correspondence
Special Assistant to the First Lady
Director of Advance for the First Lady

Hillary Clinton

Assistant to the President and Chief of Staff to the First Lady
Executive Assistant to the Chief of Staff
Deputy Assistant to the President and Deputy Chief of Staff to the First Lady
Deputy Assistant to the President and Press Secretary to the First Lady
Deputy Press Secretary (2)
Special Assistant to the First Lady
Special Assistant to the President and Social Secretary to the First Lady
Deputy Social Secretary
Assistant to the Social Secretary
Special Assistant to the Social Secretary
Director, First Lady's Correspondence

The East Wing of the White House where the First Lady's office has traditionally been located and her staff worked has been considered the social (and domestic) side of the White House, while the President had his office in the West Wing where power quite naturally was considered to be centered. "The first floor of the *West Wing* is reserved for people with real clout. The Oval Office is here, along with the White House Press Office. So are the offices of the White House chief of staff and the national security adviser.... The West Wing is where every presidential appointee longs to be. One would rather have a windowless, unventilated closet on the first floor of the West Wing than a suite in any of the other executive quarters near the White House" (McCarthy 1993).

Hillary Rodham Clinton immediately upon becoming First Lady symbolized her intention to exercise influence publicly, not privately, by taking an office in the West Wing. Her office is a "small room at the center of the second-floor work space in the West Wing of the White House, surrounded not by social secretaries but by the largely anonymous policy experts who will lay out the new administration's domestic programs" (Perry and Birnbaum 1993).

"Hillary Clinton's new job [as head of the Health Care Task Force] and her new office are a public declaration of the influence she's likely to have on the new administration and is a major change in the status of the presidential wife. In the end, she may be no more influential than Nancy, Rosalynn, or Bess, but she'll be out in the open" (McCarthy 1993). Her staff also set up offices in the Executive Office Building, another switch with the past, while the White House's social secretary and her staff maintained offices in the East Wing. Hillary Rodham Clinton was viewed by some as a quasi Chief-of-Staff. In their descriptions of the first part of the Clinton administration, Woodward (1994) and Drew (1994) often depicted Hillary as being the one to lead and focus debates about the image and the mission of the administration. She accomplished this not by acting behind the scenes but by taking part in White House staff sessions.

Not unexpectedly, the news media were fascinated by questions of Hillary Rodham Clinton's power and influence in the new administration.[2] In December prior to the inauguration, *Newsweek* focused on "Hillary: Behind the Scenes" (Clift and Miller 1992), and in February 1993, in nearly two inch headlines, it asked "Hillary's Role: The Clinton administration Is a Team Presidency. How Much Clout Does the New First Lady Have?" (Fineman and Miller 1993). *U.S. News & World Report* reported "Now the First Chief Advocate: How Hillary Clinton Plans a Bold Recasting of the Job Description for a President's Spouse" (Walsh 1993) and in February it wondered about "Co-President Clinton?" (Cooper 1993). *Time* described "The Dynamic Duo" in early January and after chronicling Hillary Rodham Clinton's personal and political career, gushed at the end of the article, "If her life continues to enrich his as much in the White House as it did in the Governor's mansion, then the country would be grateful that she drove on to Fayetteville, and will soon be headed up the Capitol steps once again, this time at Bill Clinton's side" (Carlson 1993a).

By mid-June of the first year of the Clinton administration over 100 national newspaper articles and 850 magazine stories had featured Hillary Rodham Clinton in her role as First Lady. In that same period in 1981, Nancy Reagan had fewer than 50 newspaper articles and less than 200 magazine stories. Barbara Bush had fewer than 30 newspaper and 100 magazine articles. About 300 of these 950 articles on Hillary Rodham

Clinton were editorials, whereas Nancy Reagan and Barbara Bush had been the subject of less than 25 editorials (Stuckey 1993).

Measures of public opinion usually accompanied these media reflections and analyses of the role Hillary Rodham Clinton was playing and should play. Pollsters have been particularly intrigued with the public's perception of her power and influence in the administration and with an evaluation of her role as policy adviser. Figure 5.1 traces public opinion regarding her influence in the Clinton administration over the course of the first two years of the administration, and Figure 5.2 shows perceptions of her power. During the first year approximately one-half of the public believed she had the right amount of influence. That declined to approximately one-third during the second year. Only a small minority felt she should have more influence during this period, and the percentage believing she had too much influence increased over time from approximately forty percent to over one-half.[3] Four polls between April 1993 and July 1994 asked the public to evaluate the amount of power they thought Hillary Rodham Clinton had. Consistently approximately one-half thought she had the right amount, while about four in ten thought she had too much (Figure 5.2).

As the administration got underway, the public was very split on whether Hillary Rodham Clinton should be involved in policy making—49 percent said she should not be involved in policy making while 46 percent thought that she should be (Gallup, January 1993). And while in December 1992, the *Wall Street Journal* had proclaimed that Americans were comfortable with Hillary Rodham Clinton assuming a major policy advisory role, that newspaper expressed a very different view in January 1993—"Poll Shows America Is Split About Her Involvement in Major Policy Making." Asked should Hillary Clinton be involved in major policy positions, 47 percent said yes and 45 percent said no (*Wall Street Journal*/NBC News January poll). And *US News & World Report* found people fairly evenly split as to whether Hillary Clinton's playing a major role in advising her husband about appointments and politics would help or hurt his Presidency—47 percent said she would help, 40 percent said she would hurt (Walsh 1993). (This question was not addressed in personal terms; some respondents could have been responding to general impressions of how others would view her role.)

Further, Gallup found that after nine months in the White House, including leadership on the Health Care Task Force, a position in which she primarily had received praise (see discussion below), and having obtained an overall positive image as First Lady (Chapter 4), absolutely no change had occurred in the percentage of the people who felt she should be actively

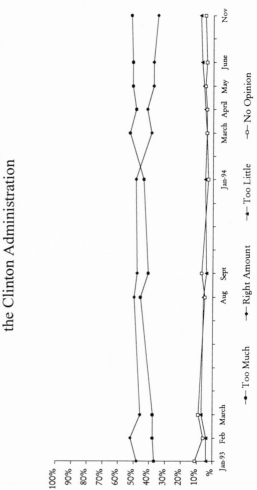

Figure 5.1 Public Opinion of the Amount of Hillary Clinton's Influence in the Clinton Administration

Figure 5.2 As first lady, do you think Hillary Rodham Clinton has too much power, about the right amount of power, or too little power?

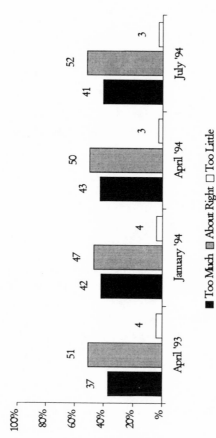

involved in policy making: nearly one-half (49 percent) at the end of September said she should not be involved in policy making (the same percentage as in January), and 41 percent felt she had too much influence in the Clinton administration. Thus, while they seemed to be quite favorably impressed with Hillary Rodham Clinton in her role as First Lady, the public still seemed to be grappling with the notion of a new type of First Lady and the idea of her being a prominent adviser to her husband.

But by the end of the first year and beginning of the second year of the administration, Hillary Rodham Clinton had obtained high approval for the way she was "handling her duties as an advisor to the President" (Times Mirror, 12/1993). A majority credited her with helping the President rather than hurting him, did not believe he was too dependent on her for policy decisions and did not believe she had too much power (Walsh, Cooper, and Borger 1994).

Thus, at this point in the administration, Hillary Rodham Clinton seemed to be successfully cultivating public acceptance for a First Ladyship as a public policy and political position. Even former President Richard Nixon had changed his mind from his negative reference in the early days of the 1992 campaign.   In February 1993 on the *Today Show*, he stated:

> if I wouldn't criticize Bill Clinton I certainly wouldn't take on Hillary, because she is a very intelligent, very strong, very effective First Lady. I think it's very appropriate for her to do what she believes is the right thing to do.... [A]s far as Hillary Clinton is concerned, with her great abilities, her intelligence and her strong beliefs, she can be a very effective help to her husband, the president, and I think the American people will like that. (As quoted in Jamieson 1995.)

This acceptance of her transformation of the First Ladyship is important. But we need to keep in mind that she had also *not* achieved it at the expense of not observing the traditional hostess role of the First Lady. She worked to ensure that the latter aspect of her position received prominent media attention along with her quasi "Chief-of-Staff" and policy maker roles. (See e.g., Drew 1994). She had striven to be successful at both tasks and she seemed to be succeeding. But it did not last.

This acceptance and support faded in 1994 as the Clintons became caught up in accusations surrounding investments in the Whitewater Development in Arkansas and as policy conundrums befell the administration. In the midst of major media attention to the Whitewater affair in the spring of 1994, a majority (53 percent) decided Hillary Rodham Clinton had too much influence as opposed to only 39 percent who felt she had the right amount (Gallup Poll, March 8, 1994), although a majority still maintained that she helped rather than hurt the administration (*Newsweek* poll, 3/1994). Negative opinions about her influence receded slightly by mid-April when 49 percent responded that she had too much influence and 42 percent said she had the right amount. And Gallup reported that "Hillary Clinton Maintains Public Support.... In the aftermath of an unprecedented televised press conference, Hillary Rodham Clinton receives strong support from the American public" (Moore and Saad 1994). But as we saw in Chapter 4, her popularity continued on a downward slope after this time. In April, Gallup reported that only 35 percent of the public believed Hillary Clinton is "knowledgeable and experienced and should be actively involved in policy-making," while "62 percent believed she "was not elected by the American people and, therefore, should not be actively involved in policy-making," a devastating critique.

Her troubles led pollsters again to query the public about the appropriateness of a First Lady undertaking a policy-making role. Fifty-five percent believed it was not appropriate for First Ladies to take on specific policy responsibilities in a *Newsweek* poll in March 1994. A similar percentage (56 percent) agreed when CBS repeated the question in December 1994. And Harris found that a near majority (46 percent) believed that Hillary Rodham Clinton's public role in making and promoting administration policies was larger than it should be for the wife of the president, while 31 percent felt it was just right.

The following questions illustrate the public's responses to Hillary as a policy advisor to the President.

1. Which one of the following statements comes closer to your view:
Hillary Clinton is knowledgeable and experienced and should be actively involved in policy-making–or–Hillary Clinton was not elected by the American people and should, therefore, not be actively involved in policy-making?

	1/29/93	9/29/93	4/22/94
Should be involved	46%	47%	35%
Should not	49	49	62
No opinion	5	3	

2. NBC News: Do you believe Hillary Clinton should or should not be involved in the development of major policy positions in the Clinton Administration?

	Jan 1993	Mar 1993
Should be involved	47%	48%
Should not be involved	45	45
Not sure	8	7

3. ABC News/*Washington Post* 11/11/93: Just your best guess, would you say that Hillary Clinton has too much influence over (President) Bill Clinton, not enough influence, or what?

Too much	52%
Not enough	10
About right	33 (vol)
No opinion	5

4. Times Mirror, 12/2/93: Do you approve or disapprove of the way Hillary Clinton is handling her duties as an advisor to the President?

Approve 59%   Disapprove 28%   Don't know/refused 13%

5. *U.S. News* 1/17/94: Do you agree or disagree with the following statements about Bill Clinton? President Clinton depends too much on his wife Hillary when it comes to policy decisions?

Agree strongly	22%
Agree somewhat	14
No difference (vol.)	1
Disagree somewhat	23
Disagree strongly	32
Unsure	9

6. *Newsweek*, March 1994:

a. On balance, do you think Hillary Clinton has helped or hurt Bill Clinton's presidency?

Helped	51%
Hurt	34
Neither (vol.)	5
Don't know	10

b. Do you think it is appropriate for Bill Clinton to appoint Hillary Clinton to help create specific administration policies, or shouldn't first ladies take on specific policy responsibilities?

Appropriate 37%   Not for first ladies 55%
Don't know   7%

c. Thinking about Hillary Clinton's public role in making and promoting administration policies, do you think it is... about right for the wife of a president, larger than it should be, or smaller than it should be?

About right 31%   Larger 46%   Smaller 11%

7. Gallup, 3/7/94: Do you think Hilary Clinton's influence has been generally positive, or generally negative on the Clinton administration?

Generally positive	65%
Generally negative	32
Mixed (vol)	2
Don't know	2

8. Harris, July 1994: Overall, do you think Hillary Rodham Clinton's influence on the president's decisions is very good, somewhat good, somewhat bad, or very bad?

	April 1994	July 1994
Very good	22%	21%
Somewhat good	46	44
Somewhat bad	15	16
Very bad	12	11
Not sure	5	8

9. CBS, 11/94: Do you think it is appropriate for President Bill Clinton to appoint Hillary Clinton to help create specific administration policies, or shouldn't first ladies take on specific policy responsibilities?

Appropriate	37%
Not for first ladies	56
Don't know	7

Group Support for a Policy-Making Role for the First Lady

Multivariate analyses regarding attitudes concerning the First Lady's influence and policy-making role not unsurprisingly show the same group support and opposition to Hillary Rodham Clinton's being involved in policy making as was found for her favorability ratings in Chapter 4 (Table 5.1). I use two polls, one from 1993 and one from 1994, to illustrate relationships between group characteristics and support for the First Lady as policy adviser. Sex, race, and party affiliation primarily distinguish among groups in support of the First Lady being active in policy making in data from *Time* magazine collected in April 1993. For example, 69 percent of women but only 56 percent of men at that time thought it was appropriate that Hillary

Rodham Clinton's role in national policy was more prominent than any other First Lady's involvement. Seventy-seven percent of Democrats and 65 percent of independents believed it was appropriate compared with only 43 percent of Republicans.

Republicans were both the least supportive and most conflicted. While 54 percent of them thought it was inappropriate for this First Lady to have a more prominent role in national policy, 43 percent thought it was appropriate. Forty-one percent of Republicans believed she was having a good influence on the President, while 40 percent thought she was having a bad influence on him. These percentages suggest Republicans were particularly divided on issues of the First Lady's influence and involvement in public policy making. That division was primarily a function of differences of opinion between female and male Republicans. Fifty-four percent of the women who identified with the Republican Party believed the more prominent role Hillary was playing in national policy was appropriate compared with only 32 percent of men who identified with the Republican Party, and 50 percent of Republican women credited her with having a good influence on Bill Clinton in matters of politics and national affairs compared with 33 percent of male Republicans. Male independents and male Democrats were also less supportive than their female counterparts, but the differences were not as great as that between the sexes within the Republican Party.

As noted earlier, positive perspectives on Hillary Rodham Clinton's involvement in public policy making declined during the second year of the administration. In the April 1994 Gallup Poll, only 35 percent of the respondents supported the idea that she was knowledgeable and experienced and should be actively involved in policy making, and 51 percent believed she had too much influence in the administration. Even close to one-half of the Democrats (45 percent) felt she should not be actively involved in public policy making, although only 27 percent of them believed she had too much influence in the administration. But partisanship and sex continued to separate supporters from nonsupporters much more than other sociodemographic factors (Table 5.1).

Table 5.1 Multivariate Analyses of Group Support for the First Lady's Involvement in Policy Making

	Time Apr '93			Gallup Apr '94	
	Q1	Q2	Q3	Q1	Q2
Sex	.10[a]	.54[c]	.78[c]	.52[b]	.44[a]
Education	.04	-.01	-.02	.19	.20[a]
Age	.03	.01	.07	-.01	-.02[b]
Income	.01	-.04	.01	-.00	.02
Race	.04	.60	1.08[a]	.52	.01
Democrat	.20[c]	.51[a]	.44		
Republican	-.20[c]	-.90[c]	-1.17[c]		
Party				.53[c]	.50[c]

[a] p>.01

[b] p>.001

[c] p>.001

Standardized regression coefficients are reported in *Time* Question 1; questions 2 and 3 are logit regression coefficients.

Time questions

Q1. As you may know, Hillary Rodham Clinton is playing a prominent role in health care policy and other domestic issues in the Clinton administration. How much confidence do you have in her ability to handle those issues—a lot of confidence, only some confidence, or no confidence at all?

Q2. Hillary Rodham Clinton's role in national policy is more prominent than any other First Lady's involvement in policy. Do you think this is appropriate or inappropriate?

Q3. Do you think Hillary Rodham Clinton has had a good influence or a bad influence on Bill Clinton in matters of politics and national affairs?

Gallup questions

Q1. In your opinion, does Hillary Clinton have too much, too little, or the right amount of influence in the Clinton administration?

Q2. Which one of the following statements comes closer to your view? 1. Hillary Clinton is knowledgeable and experienced and should be actively involved in policy-making, or 2. Hillary Clinton was not elected by the American people and should, therefore, not be actively involved in policy-making.

In the Gallup Poll, party is a five point variable running from Republican, independent leaning Republican to Democrat.

Hillary Rodham Clinton and the Health Care Task Force

In the first week of his administration, the President appointed Hillary Rodham Clinton head of his Task Force on Health Care Reform. Other First Ladies, most notably Rosalynn Carter, had had their own public policy projects. But never before had a First Lady been put in charge of a major administrative initiative. Public reaction would be crucial to her success and for the institutionalization of a major policy-making role for Presidential spouses (if they desired one).

Pollsters quickly moved to gauge public opinion regarding this appointment. They asked whether it was appropriate to appoint her, what difference it would make in actually reforming the health care system, and what kind of a job she was doing. Polls showed early support for her assuming this job. Approximately six out of ten Americans either approved, supported, or thought it was appropriate for the President to name her as head of the Health Care Task Force, while about three in ten either opposed, disapproved, or thought it was inappropriate to have made this appointment. The following questions show how the various polls asked the public what they thought about Hillary's role in health care reform.

---

1. Gallup, 1/29/93: As you may know, President Clinton has appointed Hillary to head his task-force on health care reform. In your opinion, is this an appropriate position for a First Lady, or not?

Yes 59%   No 37%   Don't know 4%

2. Yankelovich variation (Apr 28 '93)

Appropriate 58%   Inppro. 38%   Don't know 4%

3. CBS, 2/1993:

a. Bill Clinton has named Hillary Clinton to chair his health care commission. Do you think Hillary Clinton is qualified or not qualified to do this job?

Qualified 61%   Not qualified 22%   Dk 17%

b. Do you think it was appropriate for Bill Clinton to appoint Hillary Clinton to chair his health commission or shouldn't first ladies take on specific policy responsibilities?

Appropriate	59%
Shouldn't take responsibility	33
Don't know	8

4. Los Angeles Times, 2/93: Do you approve or disapprove of Clinton's decision to appoint his wife Hillary as head of the presidential task force on health care reform? Do you approve or disapprove strongly or do you approve/disapprove somewhat?

Approve strongly	39%
Approve somewhat	24
Disapprove somewhat	8
Disapprove strongly	23
Don't know	6

5. NBC, 3/93: Do you approve or disapprove of the selection of Hillary Rodham Clinton to head President Clinton's health care task force?

Approve 54%   Disapprove 37%   Not sure 9%

6. Market Opinion Research, 2/93: Do you support Hillary Rodham Clinton's appointment to head the task force on health care reform?

Support 67%   Oppose 25%   Don't know 8%

7. *Newsweek*: Do you approve or disapprove of (President) Bill Clinton naming his wife, Hillary, to lead administration efforts to reform the country's health care system?

	Feb 1993	Sept 1993
Approve	61%	56%
Disapprove	32	38
No opinion	6	

8. National Association of Children's Hospitals and Related Institutions, 1993: As a nationally-known attorney and wife of the governor, Hillary Clinton fought for important reforms in Arkansas. Recently there has been a lot of talk about Hillary Clinton heading up the president's task force on health care reform. Because of her strong background in working for reform, it is expected that she will work diligently to push the task force toward making recommendations. From what you know, do you favor or oppose Hillary Clinton heading up the health care task force? And do you feel strongly or not so strongly about that?

Strongly favor	31%	4%
Somewhat favor	44	38
Somewhat oppose	10	11
Strongly oppose	9	11
Don't know	7	7

The public also initially expressed confidence in her ability to handle the job. By the time she appeared to testify before House and Senate committees about the administration's health care plan at the end of September, 60 percent approved of her handling of health care policy, while 29 percent disapproved; 74% said she was doing an excellent or pretty good job.

The headline in Gwen Ifill's special to the *New York Times* on September 22, 1993, ran "Role in Health Expands Hillary Clinton's Power." Ifill declared that

> Mrs. Clinton is solidifying her position as the power beside, rather than behind, the throne. In doing so, Mrs. Clinton has completed a remarkable public relations transformation,

turning the personal qualities that were considered political
liabilities in the Presidential campaign into political assets
now.... Mrs. Clinton has no intention of fading away as health
care takes center stage, even if anyone were to allow her such
a luxury. Mr. Clinton and his advisers have long believed that
they have a valuable asset in Mrs. Clinton, and they hope to
use the talent for persuasion and politics she has displayed in
dealing with members of Congress to keep the outline, if not
the specifics, of the health care plan largely intact... no
previous First Lady has occupied center stage so aggressively
or disarmed her critics more effectively. And with each
success, her role has been expanded far beyond that of
previous Presidents' wives.

Ifill went on to cite the latest poll results to support her case. Support
plummeted to 47 percent in early April 1994 (Gallup Poll) after the plan had
undergone enormous attacks, and White House attention had been diverted
by the Whitewater affair and foreign policy problems. In the same poll, 47
percent expressed disapproval of the way Hillary Clinton was handling
health care policy. In July 1994, Harris found a majority still giving the First
Lady high marks with 54 percent saying she had been doing an excellent or
good job, but this represented a substantial drop-off from his earlier findings.

As the health care debate continued to be played out in the 103rd
Congress (and ultimately ended in defeat for the Clintons), a majority still felt
Hillary Clinton was helping to improve the nation's health care system (55
percent), while 36 percent believed she was hurting efforts. The public was
also divided on whether putting Hillary Clinton in charge of it had made
health care reform more likely, less likely, or hadn't made any difference—24
percent said she had made health care reform more likely, 35 percent said
less likely, and 38 percent said no difference.

In November 1994, the White House announced that Hillary Rodham
Clinton would no longer head the Health Care Task Force. The president's
wife and her task force had created an enormously complex scheme to
revamp the health care system in the United States. They had developed
much of it in secret, although the First Lady had traveled extensively around
the country listening to and talking with American citizens as she led the
Task Force. Secrecy and complexity had worked against the ability of the
Clintons to sell the plan.

In November 1994, CBS asked in a national poll, "Do you think
having Hillary Clinton chair the health care reform commission was one of

the reasons why Congress did not pass health care reform legislation last year, or don't you think so?" The public was quite split on assigning the First Lady blame for this failure—43 percent responded it was one of the reasons, while 49 percent said it was not one of the reasons. According to Julia Malone (1994), "A majority, 56 percent, say first ladies should not take on policy roles. But most don't blame Hillary Clinton's role for the administration's failure to get health reform through Congress." The following questions show the poll results on assessment of her performance as chair of the Health Care Task Force.

---

1. *Newsweek*, 2/93: Do you think Hillary Clinton will do a good job coming up with a health care plan, or not?

> Yes   62%   No   21%

2. *Time*, 5/10/93: How much confidence do you have in Hillary Clinton's ability to handle her role in health-care policy and other domestic issues?

> A lot 33%   Some 49%   None 16%

3. Market Opinion Research: Hillary Rodham Clinton heads the task force for health care reform. Do you approve or disapprove of her performance?

	Jan. 1993	April 1993
approve	67%	53%
disapprove	25	20
don't know 8		27

4. CBS: Do you think with Hillary Clinton chairing the commission, health care reform is more likely, less likely or won't that make much difference?

	Feb	March	Aug
More likely	45%	46%	34%
Less likely	6	7	11
Won't make much difference	40	39	50
DK/NA	9	8	5

5. CNN/*USA TODAY*: Do you approve or disapprove of the way First Lady Hillary Clinton is handling health care policy?

	9/12/93	9/28/93	4/22/94
Approve	50%	60%	47%
Disapprove	33	29	47

6. Harris: How would you rate the job Hillary Rodham Clinton has done in developing and presenting the President's health plan—excellent, pretty good, only fair or poor?

	10/10/93	11/11/93	7/25/94
Excellent	36%	24%	18%
Pretty good	38	44	36
Only fair	17	21	23
Poor	7	9	19

7. CBS, Nov. 94: Do you think having Hillary Clinton chair the health care reform commission was one of the reasons why Congress did not pass health care reform legislation last year (1994), or don't you think so?

One of the reasons	43%
Not one of the reasons	49
Don't know	8

Perhaps the Clinton administration erred in appointing the First Lady head of the Health Care Task Force. A number of issues must be addressed in assessing this problem such as Hillary Rodham Clinton's abilities and credentials as opposed to those of others who might have taken on the task, the political realities of the situation, its implications for the position of First Lady, and its effect on Hillary Rodham Clinton as a political leader (and on Bill Clinton). While I will discuss this problem, it remains for others more conversant with the intricacies of the political process surrounding the administrative and legislative trip health care reform took to assess some of these issues for a greater understanding of presidential policy making.

Since health care reform was a major priority of the administration and it would be a complex process, it was important that the President move fast on the issue and be able to generate a public focus on it. A health care policy expert might be able to sort through the thorny policy problems surrounding the issue and a Washington political expert might be able to deal best with the process of mobilizing support within Washington, i.e., getting the votes in Congress for passage. It is unlikely, however, that policy and political expertise would be combined in the same person. According to news accounts, Clinton had considered Vice-President Al Gore for the job, who turned it down, and Senator Bill Bradley, who felt it was an inappropriate role to assume (Woodward 1994). Clinton was reported to be unhappy prior to the inauguration with what he was hearing from advisers about the possibilities of achieving the type of reform he desired. Thus, to push what he wanted and to get the national focus it needed, he turned to his wife to lead the effort (Rosenblatt and Chen 1993; Pear 1993.) The appointment won initial praise in editorials around the country, and as we have seen, the people were supportive. (See, e.g., the *Miami Herald*, January 24 and the *Hartford Courant*, January 24.) But critics suggested that the appointment was an error because the President would be unable to fire the First Lady if she did not produce a successful plan and that there would be no accountability for her actions (Perry and Birnbaum 1993).

Health care reform ran into a number of difficulties. The President was unable to focus his legislative effort on it and develop his own political strategy to push it forward, and too many other issues made their way to the front of the President's agenda. The Clintons were also weakened by the reemergence of the Whitewater affair in early 1994. Both the President and the First Lady needed to maintain a high level of national support for themselves if they were to get Congress to focus on and pass this complex piece of legislation. Their plan has also been criticized for being too complex, and the process they established for creating and promoting it was not sensitive to the needs of others. Their own mistakes weakened their ability to achieve health care reform. Hillary's suspicion of the press and inability to engage the media became a problem.

Hillary publicly accepted some blame for the demise of the health care proposal. She believed she failed to anticipate the intensity and effectiveness of the opposition and did not realize that the complexity of the administration's original plan could work against it. She also noted her failure to be more open with the press (Clymer 1994). The Clintons can be legitimately criticized for the plan they constructed and the process they chose to make it law.

The failure even to get a vote on the floor of either house of the national legislature and the criticism of Hillary Rodham Clinton in the health care plan's demise will make it very unlikely that a First Lady will be assigned a similar task in the near future. First Ladies will be hesitant to play such a prominent role and will more likely revert to private influence. But before the idea of giving the First Lady a specific public responsibility in an administration is consigned to the "ash bin" of history, one first has to evaluate the dire predictions aimed at the gamble President Clinton took in appointing his wife to head the Health Care Task Force. While the First Lady was certainly hurt by her failure and her performance can be faulted, responsibility should fall on both Clintons for not being more politically astute as they developed their plan. The continued spotlight the administration's opponents kept on the Whitewater affair and media attention to it during crucial days of lobbying for the health care plan were major factors in weakening the Clintons' ability to focus attention on the proposed plan. President Clinton also failed to limit his agenda and make this problem his top priority.

If health care reform had passed Congress, the First Ladyship would have been transformed. The polls showed that the administration did not have to battle public opinion for the First Lady to be able to do her assigned job—the public supported her in this role and had confidence in her ability to do the job—and even in the end the public did not seem overwhelmingly opposed to her efforts. She became a target for the political opposition in the 1994 election, with hatred of her even becoming a marketing concept (*New York Times* 1994) and that was a burden on an already reeling administration. She was burned in effigy by tobacco farmers and became a target of the right-wing militia, who accused her of being a "doctrinaire Marxist who has recruited 'other American-hating subversives' for key administration posts who communes with the spirit of Eleanor Roosevelt" and has taken the lead in "big government plans to control people's lives " (See Egan 1994; Quindlen 1994b).

The debate opened once again as to what the role of First Lady should be and how Hillary Rodham Clinton should perform in that position. I will reflect on and assess the issues surrounding this debate in the concluding chapter after discussing two other aspects of Hillary Rodham Clinton on which pollsters focused.

Notes

1. White House Office organizational charts which are available for the Carter, Reagan, and Bush administrations include The Office of the First Lady in them. See Heclo and Salamon (1981) for the Carter administration chart and Edwards and Wayne (1985) for the Reagan administration chart. The Bush administration chart was made available by the Chief Clerk's Office in the White House. No organizational chart is available for the Clinton administration.

2. Even the move into an office in the West Wing was the subject of a national poll question. NBC/*Wall Street Journal* asked in January 1993, "The Clinton Administration is considering moving the reporters who cover the President out of their work space in the White House. The reason for this move would be to make room for Hillary Clinton and her staff to work in closer proximity to President Clinton. Do you approve or disapprove of this move?" Thirty-nine percent approved and 46 percent disapproved. Seven percent volunteered that it did not matter.

3. An ABC News/*Washington Post* poll in November 1992 suggested that the people thought she had too much influence. In this poll a majority (52 percent) believed she had too much influence over the President, while one-third thought she had the right amount, and 10 percent felt she did not have enough influence. Question wording is once again an important factor which can explain the divergent result of this poll compared with those of Gallup and NBC. In this poll, one had to volunteer the response that she had the right amount of influence whereas the others included that response option in the question.

CHAPTER 6

Personality and Political Leadership

The poll questions that have been examined in this study so far have focused on Hillary Rodham Clinton's role in her husband's administration. But we must also remember that the Clintons in the early stages of the 1992 election promoted the notion that having Hillary close to the center of political power was an important aspect of their quest for the presidency. She had been viewed as a political figure in her own right. Although she never ran for public office herself, she has had a long political and policy- making career. It was not just her relationship to Bill Clinton that made her a political figure although it structured the development of her political life. She had developed a political personality on her own. Pollsters have recognized this to a degree, occasionally seeking the public's pulse regarding her as a political leader. Note that Yankelovich was asking the public what they though of Hillary Clinton as a candidate for President as early as the winter of 1992.

A near majority (47 percent) in a September 1993 Gallup Poll recognized Hillary Rodham Clinton as being qualified to be President someday, and over one-third (36%) said they personally would like to see her run for President. Whether one would consider these numbers a strong or a weak base of support is rather subjective. An equal percentage thought she was not qualified, and a majority did not favor her running for President.

Whatever hesitancy the public had about Hillary's ability to be President, they were supportive of the idea of her serving in a White House position during the first year of the administration. Asked whether they agreed with the statement "She would be qualified to serve in a high White House position, even if her husband were not President," 41 percent strongly agreed, 30 percent moderately agreed, 11 percent moderately disagreed, and 16 percent strongly disagreed in the same September 1993 Gallup Poll. Support declined, however, in March 1994 to 59 percent agreeing and 39 percent disagreeing as her negatives began to rise with increased media attention to the Clintons' involvement in the Whitewater Development Corporation.

Outside of the time frame of this study but still relevant for our consideration of Hillary Rodham Clinton as a political leader, the *Washington Post* in October 1995 asked a national sample of Americans to rate the leadership abilities of several past and present political figures (Broder 1995). The response categories given to respondents were outstanding, above average, average, below average, and poor. Hillary Clinton was rated as outstanding or above average by 36 percent, average by 33 percent, and either below average or poor by 28 percent. In comparison, Bill Clinton was rated as outstanding or above average by 25 percent, average by 44 percent, and below average or poor by 30 percent.

The poll questions follow on the subject of Hillary's rating as a political leader.

---

1. *Time*, 2/92: From what you know of Hillary Clinton, do you think she has what it takes to be President of the United States, or don't you think so?

Has what it takes	19%
Does not have it	40
Not sure	14

2. Gallup, 9/29/93: Would you, personally, like to see Hillary Clinton run for President someday, or not?

Yes	36%
No	56

3. Gallup: Do you think Hillary Clinton is qualified to be president of the United States someday, or not?

	9/29/93	1/15/94
Yes, qualified	47%	45%
No, not qualified	45	50

4. Gallup: Please tell me whether you strongly agree, moderately agree, moderately disagree, or strongly disagree with the following statement about Hillary Clinton. She would be qualified to serve in a high White House position, even if her husband were not President.

	9/93	3/94
Strongly agree	41%	32%
Moderately agree	30	27
Moderately disagree	11	13
Strongly disagree	16	26
Don't know/refused	3	2

5. Yankelovich, Feb. 1994: Which of the following apply and which do not apply to Hillary Rodham Clinton?...Made things better for women by setting an example as a leader.

Apply 63%   Does not apply 29%   Not sure 8%

Personal Qualities

In addition to her actions and leadership potential, Hillary Rodham Clinton's personal character and qualities have been the subject of polls. She has been "dissected" as no other First Lady. We might have expected First Ladies' personalities to have been the subject of polls given a traditional concern with their characters, but prior to Hillary Rodham Clinton that seemed not to be the case. The broad range of aspects of her personality inquired about in the various polls reflects the intersection between the personal and public domains of the First Lady role. I have somewhat arbitrarily grouped the polled characteristics in Table 6.1 into three categories: 1) traditional, expressive traits (both positive and negative characteristics) such as warmth and friendliness and characteristics of motherhood, 2) more political traits such as toughness, ambition, manipulation, and 3) more instrumental public and policy-oriented characteristics, such as liberalism and feminism.

Hillary Rodham Clinton was already etching a strong picture in the minds of the voters early in the 1992 campaign. In *Vanity Fair*, Gail Sheehy reported the results of an early national poll (March 27-29, 1992) of perceptions of the Democratic candidate's wife,

55 percent think she is an asset to her husband's campaign: 24 percent think she's a liability. .... Those surveyed use the following descriptions of Hillary: intelligent (75 percent); tough-minded (65 percent); a good role model for women (48 percent); a feminist in the best possible sense (44 percent). The negatives: power-hungry (44 percent); too intense (36 percent); a wife who dominates her husband (28 percent).

As Table 6.1 indicates, during the campaign and in the first year of the administration, the public primarily attributed positive traits to Clinton as well as strong political ones. She was viewed as intelligent, (40% thought her smarter than her husband), ambitious, and tough, but also warm and likeable or friendly. In its January 1993 poll, Gallup found that 79 percent of respondents felt "intelligent" strongly applied to her, and 78 percent felt "ambition" strongly applied. Forty-two percent felt "warm and friendly" strongly applied. A majority also thought she cared about people like themselves, shared their values, and was a good role model for girls and women in general. She has also been viewed as being power hungry and manipulative, but in a *Time*/CNN poll in July 1992, 56 percent of the people stated that they thought she was *not too* ambitious to make a good First Lady, while 21 percent felt she was *too* ambitious. And in a March 1993 poll, Gallup reported that 60 percent of the people felt she inspired confidence, and 67 percent viewed her as an "effective manager." Overall, she scored high on the more expressive characteristics. She has also scored fairly high on more masculine characteristics such as effective manager, not always in a negative sense, although a reservoir of negativity is present. The public also see her as being more liberal than her husband and certainly a feminist. But in a February 1994 poll, *Time* magazine found that 63 percent felt she "made things better for women by setting an example as a leader," while for 29 percent this statement did not apply to her. In June 1994, 62 percent said HRC was a positive role model for American women, and 32 percent said she was not (NBC News/*Wall Street Journal* poll).

The Whitewater affair took a toll on positive ratings of these qualities. The difficulties arising from previous financial involvements pushed favorable ratings on those characteristics downward, especially the qualities of honesty and trustworthiness, which declined from 82 percent when she first entered the White House to a bare majority—52 percent—in April 1994. In June 1994, NBC News/*Wall Street Journal* reported 42 percent believed she was either very or mostly honest, while 55 percent thought she was either just somewhat honest or not very honest. And in a March 1994

Yankelovich poll for *Time* magazine, 54 percent responded that the phrase "someone I admire" did not apply to Hillary Rodham Clinton.

Table 6.1 Personal Qualities—Percent Who Agreed

	Time/CNN 7/8-92	Gallup* 1/93	Time 4/93	Gallup 9/93	Time 2/3-94	Gallup 3/4-94
Expressive Traits						
Honest & trustworthy		82%				56/51%
Warm and friendly/likeable		81	71			65
Pushy/too pushy	29/35	61	52	46	54/52	
Shares your values		64				50/46
Someone I admire	41/40				46/42	
Doesn't pay enough attention to her family	14					
Good role model for girls/young people	62/55		61		64/61	
Good role model for mothers				61		
Good role model for American women		77		67		
Cares about people like you/your needs		73				61/58
Cares about older Americans						57

Table 6.1 Personal Qualities – Percent Who Agreed, Cont'd.

	Time/CNN 7/8-92	Gallup* 1/93	Time 4/93	Gallup 9/93	Time 2/3-94	Gallup 3/4-94
Political Traits						
Intelligent	80/82	95	91		93/91	
Ambitious		94				
Tough		84				
Power-hungry		59				
Manipulative		54				
Too ambitious	21					
Smarter than Bill						40
Inspires confidence						60
Doesn't pay enough attention to her family	14/14					
Instrumental Traits						
Effective manager						67
A feminist		76				76
Too strong a feminist				41		
More liberal than husband				56		59/56
Too liberal				41		
New kind of Democrat			75			
Puts country's interests ahead of politics	52			62		50

Group Evaluations of Hillary's Personal Characteristics

Following the pattern I have constructed in earlier chapters, I have sought to explain variation in opinions about Hillary's character traits using the standard sociodemographic model plus partisanship. Data from several of the surveys allow us to examine the strength of these relationships. From each data set additive indices were created of the character traits asked about in the survey. Partisanship is by far the largest predictor of perceptions of her character with Democrats having positive opinions and Republicans being negative across the surveys (Table 6.2). For example, only 26 percent of Republicans characterized her as honest in Gallup's April 1994 poll compared with 49 percent of independents and 76 percent of Democrats. She "shared their values" with only 23 percent of Republicans but with 74 percent of Democrats.

Men viewed her in a less flattering light than women. Men and women were about equally likely to view her as a good role model for young women in the *Time* magazine poll of April 1993 (74 percent—women, 72 percent—men), while men were considerably less likely to see her as someone they admired (58 percent—women, 45 percent—men). Differences in perceptions between the sexes ranged across the items from 2 percent to 13 percent. Other demographic characteristics had little predictive value regarding Hillary Rodham Clinton's character traits. Thus, overall sex and partisanship has predicted Hillary's popularity, acceptance of her taking on a public policy advisory role in the administration as shown in earlier chapters, and evaluation of her personal characteristics as described here.

Table 6.2
Multivariate Analyses of Demographics and Opinions
of Hillary Rodham Clinton's Personality*

	Time April '93	Gallup Sept '93	Gallup April '94
Sex	.12b[a]	.16[b]	.06
Age	.06	-.00	.05
Education	.02	.07	.02
Race	.09[a]	.08	.08[a]
Income	.02	NA	.05
Democrat	.20[c]	.22[c]	.32[c]
Republican	-.16[c]	-.25[c]	.20[c]
Adjusted R^2 =	.14	.20	

*See Note 1 for a description of the questions making up these indices.
a p=.01   b p=.001   c p=.0001

Whitewater and Perceptions of the First Lady's Character

The Clinton administration was dogged by many problems in its first 18 months. One major concern was the reemergence in 1994 of questions about the President and the First Lady's investments in the Whitewater real estate venture and attempts by Hillary to help a partner in that deal with legal problems his savings and loan firm was having in the mid-1980s while she was a partner in the Rose law firm and Bill Clinton was governor of Arkansas. The issue had first surfaced during the 1992 campaign. New questions also emerged about Hillary Rodham Clinton's trading in the commodities' market in the late 1970s. These allegations hurt the Clinton's credibility and resulted in the appointment of a special prosecutor to investigate them. The press (and Republicans) made a major issue of these events. Between December 1993 and mid-August 1994, the *Wall Street Journal* ran 50 Whitewater-related editorials and the *New York Times* printed at least 40 editorials mentioning Whitewater (Boylan 1995). Alicia Shepard reports that from January through March of 1994, together ABC, CBS, and NBC devoted 284 minutes to Whitewater in weekday newscasts, and during the story's peak in March the *Washington Post* published 27 front-page Whitewater stories; the *New York Times* devoted 24 stories to its front section, and the *Boston Globe* put 29 stories on page one (1994). Pollsters undertook innumerable testings of the public's response to the Whitewater events during 1994. The polls asked about people's knowledge and interest in the affair, their views of media coverage of it, importance of the issue, and opinions of the First Lady's and the President's ethical and legal behavior in the matter. I concentrate on the latter set of issues regarding Hillary Rodham Clinton here.

Between January and May 1994, approximately one-third of the public felt that she had done something illegal in the Whitewater matter. Twenty-two percent felt this way in January; that percentage increased to 37 percent at the end of March and declined slightly to 35 percent early in May. At the same time, approximately four out of ten thought she had not done something illegal. That percentage increased to a majority (51 percent) at the end of March when opinions were most polarized (with only 12 percent volunteering that they either had no opinion or were unsure). Belief in her innocence declined to 42 percent in May while uncertainty increased to 22 percent.

Between April and September 1994, CBS/*New York Times* inquired whether the public thought Bill and Hillary Clinton did or did not do something wrong in connection with the Whitewater real estate development or didn't know enough about it yet to say. With the offered option of "don't know enough," percentages believing something had or had not been done wrong declined. Mainly the public felt that they did not know enough to give an opinion. Very few immediately believed the Clintons had done something wrong as the story began to take center stage. The percentages increased some over time but never to more than three out of ten persons. Respondents were more likely to believe the Clintons had done something unethical than illegal. Polls about the First Lady's involvement in unethical or illegal activity surrounding the Whitewater Development investment ceased after September 1994.

Allegations of wrongdoing in the Whitewater real estate development and commodities trading clearly affected the ability of the Clinton administration to concentrate on promoting its public policy program in its second year. The First Lady even had to hold a press conference in April to answer questions about her involvement. In a poll taken soon after the conference, 39 percent of a national sample of adults said Hillary Rodham Clinton was telling the truth, while 41 percent said she was not, and 20 percent volunteered that they were not sure, not an overwhelming endorsement of her. Asked by Gallup in this same poll, which came closest to their view: (a) She is a highly principled person who lives by the standards she sets for others; (b) she is no better or worse than most people; or, (c) she is basically hypocritical—that is, she fails to live by the principles and standards she sets for others, 23 percent replied that they felt she was highly principled, 52 percent thought she was like most people, and 23 percent believed she was hypocritical. We can see here the polarization she has created with nearly one-quarter strongly backing her and one quarter strongly opposed. The public response to questions about the Clintons' involvement in the Whitewater Development as measured in these polls are given below.

---

1. CBS: Do you think (President) Bill and Hillary Clinton did or did not do something wrong in connection with the real estate development Whitewater, or don't you know enough about it yet to say?

	1/94	2/94	4/94	7/94	9/94
Did something wrong	17%	15%	30%	20%	28%
Didn't do something wrong	12	12	21	18	18
Don't know enough yet	68	69	45	61	51
Don't know/no answer	3	4	4	6	3

2. ABC/*Washington Post*: Again, your best guess, do you think Hillary Rodham Clinton did anything illegal in the Whitewater matter or not?

	1/94	3/94	3/94	5/94
Yes	22%	36%	37%	35%
No	43	42	51	42
No opinion, not sure	35	22	12	22

3. Harris, Feb., 1994:

a.   In relation to the Whitewater case, do you think the President (Bill Clinton) or Mrs. (Hillary) Clinton probably did something unethical or morally wrong, or not?

Probably did something unethical	47%
Probably did not	38
Not sure	14

b.   In relation to the Whitewater case, do you think that President (Bill) Clinton or Mrs. (Hillary) Clinton probably did something illegal or not?

Probably did something illegal	35%
Probably did not	45
Not sure	19

4. *Newsweek*, 3/94: From what you have seen or heard about Hillary Clinton's profitable trading in commodities in the late 1970s, do you think she was lucky and wise in her investments or took advantage of improper or unethical deals?

Lucky and wise	37%
Improper or unethical deals	32
Haven't followed closely enough to say (vol.)	15
Don't know, refused	17

5. Gallup, April, 1994: From what you have heard or read, which way do you lean? Do you think Hillary Clinton probably did something illegal, probably did something unethical, but nothing illegal, or probably did not do anything seriously wrong?

Did something illegal	15%
Something unethical, but not illegal	41
Nothing seriously wrong	40
No opinion	4

6. Yankelovich, Mar, 1994: Aside from whether her actions were legal or not, do you think [HRC] did or did not do anything unethical in these matters (the controversy over an investment they made in Whitewater Development Corporation...

Did 38%   Did not   36%   Not sure 26%

7. Yankelovich: From what you have read and heard, do you think Hillary Rodham Clinton did or did not do anything illegal in the controversy over the Clintons' investment in the Whitewater Development Corporation in Arkansas?

	March 1994	May 1994
Did	34%	35%
Did not	39	42
Not sure	27	22

8. Yankelovich, Aug. 1994: Do you believe what the Clintons have said publicly about their roles in these matters...or do you think they are hiding something?

Believe Clintons	35%
Hiding something	51
Not sure	14

Thus, as a national leader, Hillary Rodham Clinton had the ability to connect with a lot of people. Her strong personality led to a complex picture in the minds of Americans. She was perceived to possess both masculine and feminine traits, to be a leader as well as a role model for women and girls in the early days of the administration.

But her inability to put to rest allegations of wrongdoing in her career prior to entering the White House and her failure to use those leadership attributes to achieve legislative success for health care reform made it unlikely that she would continue to exert policy and political leadership. Although, if there is a second Clinton administration, she would probably be a more visible partner again and try to regain the policy leadership connection she had attained with the public in the first year of the administration. One can see her lobbying for legislation on behalf of women and children, perhaps taking a policy leadership role in the area of education, not just acting as an outside advocate but probably not assuming a formal responsibility position again.

Epilogue

The focus of this book has been on the first two years of the Clinton administration, the time in which Hillary Rodham Clinton (to this point) worked the hardest to transform the First Ladyship into a public policy advisory position with the First Lady serving as a prominent staff assistant to the President in the White House Office. But she was hindered in achieving this goal by the continuing investigation into her role in the Whitewater affair. That involvement took a renewed prominence in early 1996.

In the aftermath of the failed Health Care Task Force and the devastating midterm elections for Democrats in 1994, Hillary Rodham Clinton turned to emphasizing a role as spokesperson for outsiders, particularly women and children. She had long been involved in children's issues and while on the campaign trail in 1992 had stressed that she wished to focus on women and children during her tenure in the White House. Her return to this interest after the 1994 elections led her to travel extensively abroad. The theme of those trips was "human rights are women's rights and women's rights are human rights." She visited Pakistan, India, Bangladesh, and Sri Lanka in the spring of 1995. One favorable editorial noted that it "was easily the most meaningful international journey so far by anyone associated with the Clinton administration—or, for that matter, the Bush and Reagan administrations. In focusing attention on the condition of women in a region where their oppression remains rampant, and in speaking frankly about the positive role of U.S. development aid for the poorest nations in the world, Clinton delivered one of the most coherent and humane international policy statements since the days of Jimmy Carter" (Editorial, *The Capital Times* 1994).

She also started a newspaper column very much in the tradition of Eleanor Roosevelt that has combined advocacy of issue positions with stories of life in the White House. As one journalist has described it, the column wraps gentle political points "in a protective layer of domesticity" (Devroy 1995a). News articles talked of her "projecting a softer image" (Raum 1995) and a "softer focus" (Devroy 1995a).

There was nothing soft spoken about her human rights speech at the United Nations Conference on Women in Beijing in September 1995, however. What she would say and how she would say it were important to American diplomatic relations with the repressive Chinese government. Whether she should even attend the conference was the subject of political debate. But the First Lady gave a ringing endorsement of women's rights and strongly condemned abuses against women. She catalogued the mistreatment of women as an abuse of human rights. "It is violation of human rights when babies are denied food or drowned or suffocated or their spines broken simply because they are born girls," she stated (Tyler 1995).

Hillary Rodham Clinton has become an immensely popular figure abroad, and we should expect her to continue to use that strength as an international advocate for women's and children's rights. According to Ann Devroy in the *Washington Post*, "[If Hillary Rodham Clinton] is not widely popular at home, she is treated virtually like a folk heroine abroad, particularly by women" (1995a). An AP wire story from China during the 1995 United Nations Conference on Women's Rights reported, "While Americans debate what the first lady's role should be, women in other countries delight in her prominence. Hillary Clinton wowed the women's conference in China, where she gave an impassioned speech declaring that the time has come to stop the abuse of women around the world. Women emerging from the hall after Hillary Clinton's address were effusive with praise. 'Give 'em hell, Hillary,' women activists shouted when she showed up the next day for a speech in Huariou, 30 miles outside of Beijing. At one conference panel, she was introduced as "the first lady of the world." Many people seem to see her as the voice of women's struggle for access to education, heath care, jobs and credit, as well as freedom from violence. ... She is incredibly popular over seas, more so than at home" her aide said (*Arkansas Democrat Gazette* 1995).

By the end of 1995 the First Lady had regained a good degree of her popularity. The Times Mirror poll at the end of October found 58 percent of a national sample rating their impressions of her as either very (14 percent) or mostly (44 percent) favorable, while 48 percent were mostly (24 percent) or very (14 percent) unfavorable. And in an early December poll conducted by Yankelovich for *Time* magazine and CNN, 57 percent responded that they had a favorable impression while 33 percent were unfavorable. Whereas Ann Devroy (1995a) had reported in the *Washington Post* that in September 1995 her rating on the "temperature scale" of one to 100 was 44 percent, eight points behind the President, it had increased to 52 points in December.[2]

In January 1996, Hillary Rodham Clinton's book *It Takes a Village and Other Lessons Children Teach Us*, a discussion of children and child-rearing issues, arrived at book stores and she was to take a national tour to promote it. This undertaking was to promote the First Lady's image as a strong advocate for children and keep a high profile on a safe issue. But this effort was deeply undercut when long-missing billing records from her

Arkansas law firm suddenly turned up in the White House residence of the first family, raising questions about how much work she had done for the Madison Guaranty Savings and Loan as part of the Whitewater investigation. Copies of these billing records had long been sought by investigators in the Whitewater affair. The amount of time reported—60 hours—was open to interpretation as to whether it contradicted her earlier testimony of little involvement. The strange way in which they suddenly appeared instilled suspicions about the truthfulness of previous statements. Then she was subpoenaed to testify before a federal grand jury about these long-missing law firm billing records. It was the first time a First Lady had been forced to undergo such an ordeal.

To make matters worse for the First Lady, a memorandum by former White House staffer David Watkins came to light at the same time, strongly suggesting Hillary Rodham Clinton had been a central figure in the firing of the Travel Office staff. Mr Watkins had written "We both knew that there would be hell to pay if we failed to take swift and decisive action in conformity with the First Lady's wishes..." (Johnston 1996).

Both the media and the Senate investigating committee jumped on these discoveries and Hillary Rodham Clinton once again came under heavy criticism. At this time she was also subpoenaed to appear before a grand jury in connection with the Madison Guaranty case. Her political opponents once again vilified her, most prominently with William Safire in the *New York Times* calling her a "congenital liar" (1996). Others wondered about her unprecedented role in the Presidential advisory system and her status among the American public fell.

In January 1996, approximately 62 questions were asked of national samples of the public about Hillary Clinton, a number nearly equal to all that had been asked in 1995.[3] On January 26, *USA TODAY* in its poll of January 12-15 found 51 percent of those surveyed saying they had an unfavorable opinion of her, "the first time a majority...rated her negatively. She received her lowest favorable rating ever, at 43%" (Page 1996). Half of all women, 51 percent, gave her a favorable rating, compared with only 35 percent of men. Younger women and single women liked her most; married men and affluent men liked her least, the article reported. Black voters were much more favorable to her than whites. While the numbers in the survey were small and thus statistically less reliable, 81 percent of black women and 74 percent of black men gave her a favorable rating.

After she testified before the grand jury, only 25 percent of a national sample thought she was telling the whole truth about Whitewater while twice as many (52 percent) believed she was hiding something.[4] Several polls throughout January found that a majority believed she was lying or covering up something in the Whitewater investigation. A majority in a Yankolovich poll for *Time* magazine also thought she was lying about her role in the Travel Office firings.[5]

The backlash against Hillary has assumed cross-national implications. Tony Blair, leader of the Labour Party in Great Britain, has had to state that his wife would not be a part of his administration if he were to become Prime Minister.

> Tony Blair last night quashed suggestions that his wife, Cherie, intended to be a power behind the throne if he became Prime Minister, as Hillary Clinton has been in America. Acutely concerned at Tory attempts to portray his wife, who is widely regarded as being more left-wing than himself, as a key political force in his life, the Labour leader stressed that, as Cherie Booth, she was a successful barrister and "has no desire to do my job." .... They are aware of the way that Hillary Clinton has become a serious liability to her husband since the Whitewater scandal and her unsuccessful high-profile attempt to reform the American health care system (Shimsbury 1996). (See also Bradshaw 1996.)

I shall now conclude this study of public opinion and Hillary Rodham Clinton by reflecting upon the larger issue of the role of the First Lady in national politics given what we have learned about Hillary Rodham Clinton's experience in the first two years of the Clinton administration.

Notes

1. *Time* magazine poll April, 1993 questions "Which of the following apply and which do not apply to Hillary Rodham Clinton?... too pushy, someone I admire, a good role model for young women.

The Gallup Poll items used in the September 1993 index are: "she is a good role model for mothers," "she is a good role model overall for American women," "she is too strong a feminist," "she is a warm and likeable person," "she is too pushy." They were measured on a four-point scale from strongly agree to strongly disagree.

The Gallup Poll items used in the April 1994 index were "honest and trustworthy," "shares your values," "cares about the needs of people like you," "she is a good role model, overall, for American women," and "she is a warm and likeable person." The first three items used an applies/doesn't apply response, and the last two were measures on the four-point agree/disagree scale.

2. Wirthlin Poll.

3. These figures are based on a review of questions stored in the University of Connecticut's Roper Center on-line archive.

4. Associated Press Poll reported in the *Capital Times*, Madison, Wisconsin, February 2.

5. Yankelovich Poll for *Time* magazine, January 10 and 11th. We should also note, however, that Hillary once again was bouncing back by March of 1996. The Field Report in California reported "Most Voters Have a Positive View of Hillary Clinton. Believe She Plays a Large Role in the Administration. Her Presence Has Little Effect On Their Vote for President." According to their poll conducted in California "For every voter who has a negative view of the job she is doing as First Lady there are two who give her positive marks " (Field Poll 1996).

CHAPTER 7

Conclusion:
The First Lady and Equality for Women

What has the experience of Hillary Rodham Clinton in the first two years of the Clinton administration and the people's response to her tenure taught us about the mixing of the public and private in political leadership? How can we solve the problem of the First Ladyship? By the problem of the First Lady, I mean the cultural imposition of a role on the spouse of a political leader that constrains that individual to the performance of only limited functions and to serving as a role model for women playing a secondary role in society and which does not allow that person to achieve on her own. There is a gendered nature to that position that clashes with feminism and conflicts with women being able to achieve as individuals. Men who have served as "first spouses" to women governors have not been expected to adopt host roles in the governors' mansions or to limit their own careers. We cannot ignore the fact that it has always been a woman in this position, which has created its gendered nature and impacted on the mixing of the private and the public.

This study of Hillary Rodham Clinton in the First Ladyship has utilized public opinion data to explore the limits and possibilities of the person in this role changing its nature. In reaching some broad conclusions based on the poll results, we need to consider responses to the polls in 1993 and in 1994 as the Clintons worked to implement their program of action. The results of the public opinion polls show or, perhaps more correctly, Hillary Rodham Clinton has shown as reflected by public opinion polls that it is possible to be an activist First Lady involved in public policy making, still be fairly popular, and not be seen as inappropriately influencing the President. This conclusion is based on public opinion polls in the first year of the Clinton administration. These polls also showed that the First Lady will be viewed in partisan terms and will lose her ability to serve as a cultural consensual figure. One has to determine if that loss is worth the effort to be part of a process of bringing about policy change. The polls also show a hesitancy on the part of the U.S. public to abandon the traditional nonpolitical nature of the First Ladyship and a preference for her not being a governmental official. But at the same time, if an individual First Lady wishes to undertake a policy leadership position, the people respond positively to that effort as they did when Hillary Rodham Clinton was named head of the President's Health Care Task Force. We need to keep in mind this mixed but primarily positive response to her activities which occurred in 1993 as we assess the First Ladyship for Hillary Rodham Clinton personally and for its position in the contemporary era.

The potential in Clinton's transformation is reflected in Jamieson's conclusion that by her performance before Congress regarding the health care bill in September 1993, Clinton had led

> reporters and columnists [to inform] their readers that... [she] had widened the range of options open to future Presidential spouses.... As the debate of the Administration health care plan she helped to create comes to the fore, noted a *New York Times* caption, "Hillary Rodham Clinton is solidifying her position as power beside rather than behind, the throne." "The national consciousness has shifted, slightly but perceptible," noted Jan R. Esiner, the *Philadelphia Inquirer's* deputy editor for the editorial page. Hillary Clinton "proved the early critics wrong, and for that I believe, many women in this country are privately grateful." (1995, 47).

However, as I have chronicled, the "popular" First Lady became quite unpopular in the second year of the administration. The Clintons faltered both in the substance of the health care plan that they put before Congress and the process which they used to develop this plan. They allowed the political opposition to undermine their popularity in 1994 by keeping the issue of their involvement in the Whitewater development project before the public. Thus, in the end they had to withdraw their health care proposal from Congressional consideration. Since the President's wife had taken the lead in this effort, she had to share responsibility for its demise. Her popularity declined and support for an activist First Lady more generally diminished.

Would it have been better had President Clinton never appointed his wife to lead the task force? In assessing this question, we must consider implications for a changing First Ladyship if the outcome of the task force had been different; what if the Clintons had been successful in enacting into law some type of health care reform? Clearly the First Ladyship would have been transformed. The important point here is that public opinion polls showed substantial support for a person undertaking that transformation, although it also implies that she could probably only achieve a redefinition if at the same time she did not neglect or show contempt for the traditional ceremonial, hostess, and homemaker duties of the First Lady. Hillary Rodham Clinton worked hard to combine both roles, which often confused journalists covering her but probably helped to sustain her popularity.

In perspective, in some ways President Clinton's appointment of Hillary Rodham Clinton as head of the health care task force was exactly the right thing to do to move beyond the constraining of political wives to secondary roles. It allowed her to seek to accomplish something through her own abilities (which is not to ignore the political reality that other actors in the process would still respond to her in a special way because she was the wife of the President). Of course, she was given the position because she was the President's spouse, but advisers are often given positions because they are long-time confidants of the President. Personal relationships are always part of the selection of advisers as well as more "objective" credentials.[1] In Hillary's case, it was not as if the job was given to someone who had never been involved in the policy-making process and had no claim to leadership abilities other than her wedding ring as a credential, although health care was not her forte. We should recall the earlier discussion in this book that she was viewed as being qualified for a high level position in a Democratic administration if her husband had not been President.

Unfortunately for breaking the cultural constraints of the First Ladyship, Clinton failed in her effort to achieve a policy triumph for her husband and allowed herself to become a target for the political right, contributing to the undermining of her husband's ability to lead the nation. Thus, after the disastrous 1994 midterm elections for Democrats, Hillary was made to rethink her role and probably would not take on a policy-making position during the rest of the administration. She was given lots of advice in the media as to what she should do and what the First Ladyship should be about. Advice focused both on her role in this position and reflections on the First Ladyship more generally.

Supporters of an activist First Lady for the most part suggested that Hillary Rodham Clinton should continue to be a national advocate for the causes she believed in but should not attempt to be a policy maker. For example, journalist Gloria Borger speaking on *Inside Politics* suggested, "I wouldn't advise the White House to put Hillary Rodham Clinton in charge of a welfare reform task force right now, as she did for health care. But on, the other hand, I think people are also saying, being in an advisory capacity, being in an outspoken capacity—there's nothing wrong with that" (November 30, 1994).   Anna Quindlen (1994c) and Doris Kearns Goodwin (1994) advocated her becoming a spokesperson for outsiders in the spirit or style of Eleanor Roosevelt. Her public activities in 1995 indicated that is exactly the route she decided to take.

Others believe the First Lady should sacrifice any public opinions that she might have and any ideas of a political partnership to concentrate on being a nonpolitical symbol which Americans seem to need. Betsy Hart, writing in the *Rocky Mountain News*, illustrates this position, "For while the President must play politics and to a certain extent be divisive, we rely on a first spouse—until now first ladies—to unite us; to be someone we all can look to respect and claim as our own. We want the first spouse to be someone all Americans can cheer, like Barbara Bush or Jackie Kennedy. Not someone who herself (or himself) is embroiled in divisive political fights" (1994). Advocates of this position, however, fail to tell us why it is that the spouse of a chief executive must take on this role. A variant of this theme has been expressed by former First Lady Barbara Bush who said the First Lady should keep her opinions to herself as she was not elected, her husband was. The constraints on the First Lady and the imposition of a role suggested by these perspectives go against our individual achievement culture. Barbara Bush does have a point, however, if the media are only interested in the First Lady's opinions because she happens to be the spouse of the President rather than having been involved in the political process in her own right.

Others argue that the entire idea of a "First Lady" is outdated and even contrary to a democratic society. Germaine Greer, writing in *The New Republic* (1995), advocated abolishing the First Ladyship. The notion of a "First Lady" according to Greer has more to do with royalty and hereditary systems of rulership than with democracies that elect individuals to public office. "The country that pioneered democracy also invented its contradiction in the figure of the unelected First Lady. The phenomenon was created by the American newspapers that reported the first public appearances of George Washington's almost-60 year-old wife,

Martha, in 1789." Greer believes Presidents' spouses should be freed to lead private lives and pursue careers of their own: "No woman anywhere will be expected to relinquish her privacy and her own work, to diet and dress up and give interviews every day, simply because she has married a man who has a prospect of success in politics." This individualistic perspective very much represents the philosophy of the contemporary feminist movement. A.M. Rosenthal in the *New York Times* has made a similar point: "... it is a job that should not exist. It is philosophically twisted in concept and it is politically outrageous in practice. In concept, the First Ladyship is an affront to American democracy—and to American feminism" (1994).

But we have moved in the opposite direction regarding Presidents' spouses. The contemporary First Lady has an office allocated to her and a budget appropriated for her assistance by the U.S. Congress (although no salary) as a consequence of the White House Personnel Authorization-Employment Act of 1978 as discussed in Chapter 5. Thus, her position has expanded and become more formal. Even the fact that she has been given a "title," official in the sense that government manuals now list the Office of First Lady as part of the President's Office and is not just known as the wife of the President suggests a governmental position. She is assumed to have official duties. Pollsters even ask the public to evaluate the "job" she is doing. But our culture constrains those duties and confines the person in this position to seemingly nonpolitical public roles—to be first hostess. What happens when that individual, rather than desiring to be a private person perhaps with a career of her own or performing the homemaker role out of the public eye or being the first hostess, has been a political adviser and wishes to be involved in policy making? That is a real problem in our individual achievement-oriented society.

If we did away with the formal position of First Lady following Germaine Greer's call and treated the President's spouse as an individual, then perhaps she (or he) would be free to assume a political advisory position in the administration or even serve in the Cabinet if she had the professional background or political credentials to assume such a position. She could be evaluated on her own merits in the tradition of our individual achievement culture. Movement in this direction of abolishing the position of First Lady would eliminate at least to a degree the problem of mixing private and public spheres. Less of the spouse's role in governing would flow from her private relationship with the chief executive and more would come from, shall we say, public or political achievement, from her own credentials. The fact that she is the spouse becomes secondary, although of course the special intimacy of the husband and wife relationship can not be removed entirely. And the advantage she would have vis-à-vis other advisers would probably continue to cause consternation within the Office of the President. But by its nature the Office of the President is filled with jealousies and competition for influence with or without the involvement of the President's spouse.

Of course, it is unrealistic to expect that the "First Ladyship" could be banished. It was not created by an act of Congress. It is a cultural tradition that has developed over time and gradually has become institutionalized as part of government. Congress might rescind that section of Public Law 95-570, the White House Personnel Authorization-Employment Act of 1978 that authorizes funds for a Presidential spouse to assist her husband and provides a certain amount of legitimization for her office in the White House. The social apparatus of the White House rather than being institutionalized under the First Lady's domain should be reconstructed to report to the President's chief-of-staff through some line of authority. The President could organize the White House Office so that it does not include an Office of the First Lady.

It is hard to imagine, however, these actions being taken. Even with all of its cultural constraints the First Ladyship provides the individual who assumes that role through a marital relationship with a great deal of influence if she wishes to exercise it. Therefore, little incentive is present for an individual today to renounce assumption of that role. Thus, we must assess the expansion of this position and evaluate possibilities for its alteration.

Some have suggested that President Clinton raised a constitutional issue in appointing Hillary head of the Task Force in that he skirted the Bobby Kennedy law. (See, for example, Hoff 1996; Rosenthal 1994.) Since she received no pay technically he did not violate it. Also the law states that "a public official may not appoint, employ, promote, [or] advance a relative in an agency in which he is serving or over which he exercises jurisdiction or control...." But does the appointment to a staff position as an advisor within the White House, not to an executive branch agency, constitute "appointment to an agency?"

President Clinton might have shown more respect for the legislative process by speaking to the problems that law creates for Presidents, noting perhaps among other things, its limit on the President's freedom to obtain assistance from people close to him, its insult to his ability to choose competent advisors, and the ability of the U.S. public to render judgment on the President's competency to choose his assistants based on their actions. What President Clinton might have done was to raise the issue and have legislation introduced into Congress to rescind the law suggesting that it take effect after his administration. Such an action might have shown respect on his part for the lawmaking process.

The law was originally passed in spite by the Johnson administration after President Kennedy had appointed his brother to be Attorney General, a man whom Lyndon Johnson intensely disliked and viewed as a political rival. It could be pointed out that the President is free to appoint any cronies he wishes to staff positions in the White House but not his brother, uncle, or mother. He could even, one supposes, appoint his mistress but not his wife. What if Bill and Hillary were to divorce as the tabloids have occasionally suggested? Could he then appoint her to be Attorney General or Secretary of Education (maybe even as part of the divorce settlement)? Of course that seems ridiculous, but it is an extension of the logic of the prohibition of this piece of legislation on Presidential appointments. One could even take it one step further and imagine that had Bill and Hillary never gotten married but only lived as partners, he would have had no legal limitations on appointing her to an executive branch position. It is a separate question as to whether the public would have been ready to accept such a living arrangement in a Presidential candidate. But such arrangements have become more and more an accepted part of contemporary life. Finally, we need to consider the fact that Elizabeth Dole was qualified to serve as Secretary of Labor and Secretary of Transportation in previous Republican administrations but cannot do that if her husband U.S. Senator Bob Dole is elected President.

In evaluating the idea of the First Lady as playing a role as a public Presidential advisor, the issue of accountability has been raised. Some observers have suggested a lack of accountability exists when the First Lady becomes involved in public policy. For example, Maureen Dowd made this point in an October 1995 *New York Times* editorial critical of Hillary Clinton for taking on a policy-making role: "When she came to Washington, Mrs. Clinton appeared to willfully ignore the political dangers of assigning herself so much power with no accountability....She thinks Americans fear the partnership with her husband. What they really fear is a bargain that ignores accountability. It's not about being a woman. It's about not being elected." Or note Meg Greenfield's comment regarding Rosalynn Carter's public policy advisory role, "Mrs. Carter, by her very seriousness of purpose, is inviting an end to this facade of deference. She is asking to be part of the political and governing process, and the answer to whether or not she *should* do that is this: only if she agrees to make herself accountable in the ordinary way" (1977).

But does little accountability exist for a Presidential spouse who "works" in her husband's administration? What are the ways in which the First Lady can be held accountable? In advocating a role for her in the public policy-making process, we must assess the presence and effectiveness of any means by which she can be held accountable. A major element of accountability would be receiving a salary and being subject to being fired for not performing the job according to the wishes of the President. The nation has chosen not to provide a salary for the spouse of the President for the performance of her overall duties as hostess plus advisor, nor can she be paid because of the "Bobby Kennedy" law for any particular task that she undertakes for the President. No formal means of firing her exist either. But she can be dismissed from a position as Hillary essentially was from the Health Care Task Force.

Some informal ways do exist by which she can be held accountable, probably even more so than most presidential advisers. First is the fact that she is the person "closest to the President." Thus, her activities reflect most directly on him and his Presidency. Her performance will affect evaluation of him more immediately than that of any other adviser. Her incompetency, particularly given the gendered context in which it will be viewed, will harm him to a greater degree than other administration blunders. Second is the fact that the First Lady's actions receive immense press scrutiny. There is little that she could do as a public advisor that will not be publicized and analyzed in news stories, editorials, and nightly news commentary. This indirect form of accountability plays a major role in keeping the First Lady accountable for her actions. If she only advises behind the scenes within the facade of playing the hostess role, we have much less accountability. Too, it would be unnatural to expect that no Presidential spouse would offer advice and be involved in the workings of the administration. First Ladies have a long history of being engaged as political partners to their husbands.

What if we were to think of the appointment of a Presidential spouse to an advisory position as making that individual a quasi-member of the White House Office staff. I use the term "quasi" only because of the inability to pay a spouse a salary. If her advisory post were to be considered a staff position, she would be held to the same accountability standards as other staff members. (This, of course, ignores the greater reticence some might have to raise questions about the performance of the Presidential wife as opposed to that of other staff members, but such hesitation reflects back to our discussion of the First Lady as an icon that has caused problems for equality in contemporary times.)

What then are the general mechanisms for holding Presidential staff accountable? Holding Presidential staff accountable has been a source of consternation within Congress and among students of the presidency. It has not been an easily resolvable issue. (See, e.g., Hart 1987.) The potential for holding Presidential staff accountable comes primarily through Congressional oversight mechanisms. The most immediate means relevant for our purposes here is Congress's right to hold hearings and investigations into executive branch activities. According to Presidential scholar John Hart, hearings and investigations have been the most visible forms of Congressional oversight and one of the primary means by which it has held the officials who manage the departments and agencies of the executive branch accountable.

> Those whose appointments in government are established by law are expected to testify before congressional committees when asked to do so, and their testimony, and the information it provides, is considered vital to the effective performance of the oversight function. Presidential staff have been treated as an exception in this respect because of their close relationship with the President, and the doctrine of executive privilege is invoked to exclude them from the requirement to testify before Congress. The rationale for this is simply that Presidents need the best advice available, and that advice might not be given so freely if advisers were denied the protection of confidentiality and ultimately forced to account in a public forum for the advice given.

> That rationale is less applicable, and claims of executive privilege more questionable, when Presidential aides become policy makers in their own right, as has happened in recent decades (145).... Existing law makes it a misdemeanor, punishable by a fine and imprisonment, for anyone to refuse to appear as a witness if summoned by Congress and to refuse to answer any pertinent question. There is no specific exemption in the law for the Presidential staff, not even for the President's personal staff in the White House Office. In terms of the strict letter of the

law, it would seem that the Presidential staff have no right
to refuse to attend a congressional committee hearing and,
if they refused to answer any pertinent question on the basis
of executive privilege, than, because a misdemeanor would
have been committed, the matter would have to be resolved
in the courts, and it would be up to the courts to determine
the claim of executive privilege. But Congress has been
reluctant to push the issue into the courts, and the effect of
that reluctance has left the White House staff the sole
arbiters of when the doctrine of executive privilege should
be invoked (146).

In her capacity as head of the Health Care Task Force, Hillary
Rodham Clinton should have been held accountable by Congress's ability
to call her to come before them to describe and defend her actions in that
position, but as Hart has told us, Congress has been reluctant to pursue
that avenue in general to hold White House staff accountable. But it does
not follow that the First Lady is uniquely not held accountable for her
actions in this position.

In the end, to argue against the President's spouse being able to take
on a policy-making role is to constrain women from playing an equal role
in the political life of the nation. The challenge is to alter that position and
the way that we think about people in it so that spouses can achieve in
their own right whether that achievement is in pursuit of a profession or
vocation entirely on their own divorced from the Presidency or whether it
is performing a key function in the administration. How much better for
women if the spouse is not seen as manipulating policy behind the scenes
and does not have to pretend to check her brain at the door of the White
House as Hillary Rodham Clinton has noted. She should be allowed to
choose what to do with her life.

The theme of choice became a notable refrain in the public
statements of the candidates' wives in 1992 in the aftermath of Marilyn
Quayle's "essential natures" comment in her speech at the 1992
Republican convention. To calm the controversy swirling around her
earlier comment, Quayle wrote in a follow-up piece that "We don't have
to reject the prospect of marriage and children to succeed. We don't have
to reject our essential natures as women to prosper in what was once the
domain of men. It is no longer an either-or situation." According to
Barbara Bush, "everyone's different and that's a great thing." Hillary
Clinton repeated as often as possible the statement that each woman

should choose what is best for her. When asked by Larry King whether she had changed the pattern for First Ladies, Clinton responded,

> Larry, I don't think there should be a pattern. I really think that each individual ought to be free to do what she thinks is best for herself and her husband and her country. I have a lot of respect for all the women who have been in this position and I think every one of them made a significant contribution, but they may have done it in a different way.... Everybody should be permitted to be who they are" (Jamieson 1995, 44-45).

In an interview with reporters at the conclusion of her five-day Latin America tour in October 1995, Clinton reiterated this theme. "First ladies, she said, are caught in an 'inevitable double bind,' attacked if they are too active and if they are not active enough. Her plea for her successors, she said, is that they be allowed to work out any kind of conventional or unconventional role in a world where women's roles are changing. A first lady, she said, should be allowed to be an activist or 'not do anything at all'" (Devroy 1995b).

Thus, if it is accepted that every woman should choose what is best for her, then why shouldn't the First Lady be able to choose to be a political partner and policy-making adviser to the President? Why should Hillary Rodham Clinton have had to relinquish a role which she had performed in Arkansas once she moved to Washington?

What is left for us to consider is the degree to which it matters more broadly what role the spouse of the President plays and what positions she assumes in an administration. The First Lady's role has been as an icon for the ideal of American womanhood. It is steeped in the traditions of public and private that have driven political philosophy and constrained women from being able to attain individual achievement. If the First Lady becomes free of those cultural limitations and does not have to check her brain at the door of the White House, as Hillary Rodham Clinton has noted, it represents an egalitarian step forward for American women. The symbolic importance of freeing political wives would be large. It might help political husbands, also.

The vast majority of Americans express support for the idea of women in political leadership positions. In 1987, 82 percent expressed approval when asked in a Gallup poll, "If your party nominated a woman for President, would you vote for her if she were qualified for the job?"

And in another Gallup poll in 1984, 91 percent said they would vote for a woman for Congress. The debate that Hillary Rodham Clinton engendered during the 1992 Presidential campaign distracted from the record number of women running for public office that year. Some commentators derisively called it the "Year of the Wife," rather than the "Year of the Woman," which had the intended impact of hurting the cause of liberal equality for women. The debate about the political influence of the First Lady detracts from the ability of women seeking elective and appointive office. It continues to confuse the private and public and stresses gendered roles. The First Ladyship is an old-fashioned idea that conflicts with contemporary beliefs in women's equality and women's quests for political leadership. Hillary Rodham Clinton's tenure in the White House has made that very clear.

Notes

1. And ambassadors' main credential for the position often has been the amount of money they had donated to a President's campaign.

REFERENCES

Anthony, Carl Sferrazza. 1990. *First Ladies: The Saga of the Presidents' Wives and Their Power, 1789-1961*. New York: William Morrow and Company.

Anthony, Carl Sferrazza. 1991. *First Ladies: The Saga of the Presidents' Wives and Their Power, 1961-1990*. New York: William Morrow and Company.

Arkansas Democrat Gazette. 1995. "Overseas, Women See Hillary Clinton as Their Champion." September 10: 7A.

Baldrige, Letitia. 1968. *Of Diamonds and Diplomats*. Boston: Houghton Mifflin Company.

Bardes, Barbara, and Suzanne Gossett. 1990. *Declarations of Independence: Women and Political Power in Nineteenth Century American Fiction*. New Brunswick, New Jersey: Rutgers University Press.

Beasley, Maurine. 1987. *Eleanor Roosevelt and the Media*. Chicago: University of Illinois Press.

Beck, Joan. 1992. "Hillary: Powerhouse or White Housewife?" *Chicago Tribune*, November 19.

Benedetto, Richard. 1992. "Wynette Remark Shows Democrats Once Again Misread Millions." *Gannett News Service*. January 31.

Benedetto, Richard. 1993. "Activist Role Wins Approval." *USA Today*, October 1.

Boylan, James. 1995. "The Scarlet W." *Columbia Journalism Review.* January/February: 53-60.

Bradshaw, David. 1996. "Cherie's Not After My Job—That's More Tory Dirt; Blair Defends His Wife." *Daily Mirror*, April 10, Sec. A2.

Broder, David. 1992. "New Kind of Ground Rules for a First Lady." *Washington Post,* November 29.

Broder, David. 1995. "Looking for Leadership, Voter Rage Cools, Worries Remain." *Washington Post*, November 6, Sec A1.

Buhle, Mari Jo, and Paul Buhle. 1978. *The Concise History of Woman Suffrage.* Urbana: University of Illinois Press.

Burrell, Barbara. 1994. *A Woman's Place Is in the House: Campaigning for Congress in the Feminist Era.* Ann Arbor: The University of Michigan Press.

Campbell, Karlyn Kohrs. 1989. *Man Cannot Speak for Her.* Westport, Connecticut: Greenwood Press.

Campbell, Karlyn Kohrs. 1993. "Shadowboxing with Stereotypes: The Press, the Public, and the Candidates' Wives." Research Paper R-9. Cambridge, Massachusetts: John F. Kennedy School of Government.

The Capital Times. 1995. "A First Lady's Global View." April 8, Sec. A.

Carlson, Margaret. 1993a. "The Dynamic Duo." *Time*, January 4: 39-41.

Carlson, Margaret. 1993b. "At the Center of Power," *Time*, May 10: 29-36.

Caroli, Betty Boyd. 1987. *First Ladies.* New York: Oxford University Press.

Carroll, Ginny. 1992. "Will Hillary Hurt or Help?" *Newsweek*, March 30:30-31.

Castaneda, Carol, and Brian O'Donnell. 1992. "Women, Youth Rate Hillary Clinton Highest." *USA TODAY*. March 24.

Clift, Eleanor. 1992a. "Hillary Then and Now." *Newsweek*, July 20.

Clift, Eleanor, and Mark Miller. 1992. "Hillary: Behind the Scenes." *Newsweek*, December 28.

Clymer, Adam. 1994. "Hillary Clinton Says Administration Was Misunderstood on Health Care." *New York Times,* October 3.

Cohen, Richard. 1992. "The Hillary Clinton Factor." *Washington Post,* March 18.

Converse, Jean, and Stanley Presser. 1986. *Survey Questions: Handcrafting the Standardized Questionnaire*. Newbury Park, California: Sage Publications.

Cooper, Matthew. 1992. "The Hillary Factor." *U.S. News & World Report,* April 27: 32-37.

Cooper, Matthew. 1993. "Co-President Clinton?" *U.S. News & World Report*. February 8: 30-32.

Corcoran, Katherine. 1993. "Pilloried Clinton." *Washington Journalism Review*. January/February: 27-29.

CQ Almanac. 1978. Washington, D.C.: Congressional Quarterly Press.

Creager, Ellen. 1992. "Some Say She's the One Who Should Be President." *Detroit Free Press*, January 14.

Davis, Anna Byrd. 1993. "Hillary Clinton's Support Booms." *Tennessee Commercial Appeal*, March 22.

Devroy, Ann. 1995a. "First Lady's Softer Focus Follows Drop in Popularity." *Washington Post*, October 15: A1.

Devroy, Ann. 1995b. "First Lady Denounces Her Critics." *Milwaukee Journal Sentinel*, October 18: 1.

Diamond, Edwin, Gregg Geller, and Heidi Ruiz. 1993. "Watching the Hillary-Watchers. . . Shows How Coverage Has Changed." *National Journal*. April 24: 1004-5.

Dowd, Maureen. 1992. "The 1992 Campaign Trail: From Nixon, Predictions on the Presidential Race." *New York Times*, February 6, Sec. A.

Dowd, Maureen. 1995. "Return to Gender." *New York Times*, October 19.

Drew, Elizabeth. 1994. *On the Edge: the Clinton Presidency*. New York: Simon and Schuster.

The Economist, 1992. "Hillary Clinton, Trail-blazer." December 5: 30.

Edwards, George, and Stephen Wayne. 1985. *Presidential Leadership*. New York: St Martin's Press.

Egan, Timothy. 1994. "New Idaho Community Raises Neighbors' Fears." *New York Times,* October 5.

Elshtain, Jean Bethke. 1974. "Moral Woman and Immoral Man: A Consideration of the Public-Private Split and Its Political Ramifications." *Politics and Society*. 4:453-473.

Field Poll. 1996. "Most Voters Have a Positive View of Hillary Clinton. Believe She Plays a Large Role in the Administration. Her Presence has Little Effect on Their Vote for President." Press Release, March 19.

Fineman, Howard, and Mark Miller. 1993. "Hillary's Role." *Newsweek*, February 15: 18-23.

Fogarty, Thomas. 1993. "Iowans Give Thumbs Up to First Lady." *Des Moines Register*, May 3.

Foreman, Norma Ruth Holly. 1971. "The First Lady as a Leader of Public Opinion: A Study of the Role and Press Relations of Lady Bird Johnson." Ph.D. Dissertation. University of Texas, Austin.

Frisby, Michael. 1992. "Large Role for Mrs. Clinton No Longer Troubles Most Americans." *Wall Street Journal,* December 18, Sec. A6.

Gallup, George. 1939. "Mrs. Roosevelt More Popular Than President, Survey Finds." *Washington Post,* January 15.

Garment, Suzanne. 1992. "Attacking Hillary's Views is Progress." *Los Angeles Times,* August 23.

Germond, Jack, and Jules Witcover. 1993. *Mad As Hell: Revolt at the Ballot Box, 1992.* New York: Warner Books.

Goldman, Peter, Thomas M. DeFrank, Mark Miller, Andrew Murr, and Tom Mathews. 1994. *Quest for the Presidency: 1992.* College Station, Texas: Texas A & M University Press.

Goodwin, Doris Kearns. 1993. "Hillary & Eleanor." *Mother Jones,* January/February.

Goodwin, Doris Kearns. 1994. "For Roosevelt Biographer, Clinton Role Is Unwritten." *Washington Post,* November 24: B20.

Gould, Lewis. 1985. "Modern First Ladies in Historical Perspective." *Presidential Studies Quarterly* 15: 532-540.

Gould, Lewis. 1996. *American First Ladies: Their Lives and Their Legacy.* New York: Garland Publishing.

Greenfield, Meg. 1977. "Mrs. President." *Newsweek,* June 20: 100.

Greenfield, Meg. 1993. "Did She Take the Hill?" *Newsweek,* October 11: 72.

Greer, Germaine. 1995. "Abolish Her." *The New Republic,* June 26: 21-27.

Gutin, Myra. 1989. *The President's Partner: The First Lady in the Twentieth Century.* Westport, Connecticut: Greenwood Press.

Hall, Mimi. 1992. "Hillary Clinton: Asset or Liability?" *USA TODAY*, July 10.

Hart, Betsy. 1994. "How Should First Lady Be Judged?" *Rocky Mountain News*, October 20: 56A.

Hart, John. 1987. *The Presidential Branch*. New York: Pergamon Press.

Hartford Courant. 1993. "Hillary Clinton Goes to Work." January 24, Sec, C2.

Heclo, Hugh, and Lester Salamon. 1981. *The Illusion of Presidential Government*. Boulder, Colorado: Westview Press.

Hoff, Joan. 1996. "Hillary Clinton Is No Eleanor Roosevelt." *New York Times*, January 22, Sec. A.

Ifill, Gwen. 1992a. "G.O.P. Makes Hillary Clinton Issue of the Day." *New York Times*, August 13, Sec. A11.

Ifill, Gwen. 1992. "Clinton Wants Wife at Cabinet Table." *New York Times*, December 12.

Ifill, Gwen. 1993. "Role in Health Expands Hillary Clinton's Power." *New York Times*, September 22.

Jamieson, Kathleen Hall. 1988. *Eloquence in an Electronic Age*. New York: Oxford University Press.

Jamieson, Kathleen Hall. 1995. *Beyond the Double Bind*. New York: Oxford University Press.

Jensen, Faye Lind. 1990. "As Awesome Responsibility: Rosalynn Carter as First Lady." *Presidential Studies Quarterly*. 769-775.

Johnston, David. 1996. "Memo Places Hillary Clinton at Core of Travel Office Case." *New York Times*, January 1, Sec A.

Kahn, Joseph. 1992. "As Her Husband's Campaign Struggles, She Hits the Hustings in New Hampshire." *Boston Globe*, February 13.

Kerber, Linda. 1980. *Women of the Republic: Intellect and Ideology in Revolutionary America*. Chapel Hill: University of North Carolina Press.

Kerber, Linda. 1995. "A Constitutional Right to Be Treated Like American Ladies: Women and the Obligation of Citizenship." In *U.S. History as Women's History*. Ed. Linda Kerber, Alice Kessler-Harris, and Kathryn Kish Sklar. Chapel Hill: University of North Carolina Press.

Kolbert, Elizabeth. 1992. "Test Marketing a President." *New York Times Magazine*, August 30.

Kraditor, Aileen. 1965. *The Ideas of the Women's Suffrage Movement*. New York: W.W. Norton.

Lerner, Gerda. 1993. *The Creation of Feminist Consciousness*. New York: Oxford University Press.

Lewis, Anthony. 1992. "Merchants of Hate." *New York Times*, August 21, Sec. A.

McCarthy, Abigail. 1992. "They Just Don't Get It." *Commonweal*. October: 9-10.

McCarthy, Sheryl. 1993. "For Hillary, Cookie Days Are Over." *Newsday*, January, 25: 13.

McClung, Lori. 1993. "First Lady Rates High in Ohio." *Cincinnati Post*, June 7.

McRoberts, Flynn, and Jerry Thomas. 1992. "Hillary Clinton may be Candidate's Top Asset." *Chicago Tribune,* January 31: 10.

Miami Herald. 1993. "First Lady's First Job Is Vital." January 24, Sec. M.

Malone, Julia. 1994. "Hillary Clinton Is Pressured to Rethink Her Role." *Austin American-Statesman*, November 30.

Mann, Judy. 1992. "Hillary Horton?" *Washington Post*, August 21.

Mayo, Edith. 1993. "The Influence and Power of First Ladies." *Chronicle of Higher Education*. 40 September 15: A52.

Mayo, Edith, and Denise Meringolo. 1994. *First Ladies: Political Role and Public Image*. Washington, D.C.: Smithsonian Institution.

Miami Herald. 1993. "First Lady's First Job Is Vital." January 24, Sec. M.

Moore, David, and Lydia Saad. 1994. "Hillary Clinton Maintains Public Support." *The Gallup Poll Monthly*. April: 1517.

Morganthau, Tom. 1979. "The President's Partner." *Newsweek*, November 5: 36-47.

Morrison, Patt. 1992. "Time for a Feminist as First Lady?" *Los Angeles Times*, July 14, Sec. A.

Mughan, Anthony, and Barry C. Burden. 1995. "The Candidates' Wives." In *Democracy's Feast*. Ed. Herbert Weisberg. Chatham, New Jersey: Chatham House Publishers, Inc.

Neal, Stephen. 1992. "Hillary Clinton Ridicule Strikes a Sour Note." *Chicago Sun-Times,* January 31.

New York Times. 1994. "Enemies Lists." October 23: 18.

Norton, Mary Beth. 1980. *Liberty's Daughters*. Boston: Little, Brown and Company.

Okin, Susan. 1979. *Women in Western Political Thought*. Princeton, New Jersey: Princeton University Press.

Page, Susan. 1996. "First Lady: Behind the Numbers." *USA TODAY*, January 26, Sec A4.

Pear, Robert. 1993. "Hillary Clinton Gets Policy Job and New Office." *New York Times*, January 22.

Perry, James M., and Jeffrey H. Birnbaum. 1993. "'We' the President: Hillary Clinton Turns the First Lady Role Into a Powerful Post." *Wall Street Journal*, January 28, 1993.

Phillips, Anne. 1991. *Engendering Democracy*. University Park: The Pennsylvania State University Press.

Pogrebin, Letty Cottin. 1992. "Give Hillary a Break." *New York Times*, June 8.

Pollit, Katha. 1992. "Are We Ready for a First Lady as First Partner?" *Glamour*, September.

Pollit, Katha. 1993. "The Male Media's Hillary Problem." *The Nation*, May 17: 657-660.

The Public Perspective, 1993. "Hillary Rodham Clinton," July/August: 97.

Quindlen, Anna. 1994a. "Public & Private: The Cost of Free Speech." *New York Times*, February 9.

Quindlen, Anna. 1994b. "Public & Private." *New York Times*, May 7.

Quindlen, Anna. 1994c. "Time Right for Hillary to Alter Image." *Wisconsin State Journal*, October 16.

Radcliffe, Donnie. 1992. "Hillary Clinton and the Laws of the Campaign." *Washington Post*, October 30.

Raum, Tom. 1995. "Hillary Image Gets Makeover to Warm, Fuzzy." *The Capital Times*, November 29, 1.

Reed, Judith. 1993. "The First Lady." *Vogue,* 183, December: 228-33.

Roberts, Roxanne. 1993. Hillary Clinton Gets Personal." *Redbook*, March.

Rosebush, James. 1987. *First Lady, Public Wife*. Lanham, Maryland: Madison Books.

Rosenblatt, Robert, and Edwin Chen. 1993. "Clinton Seeks First Lady's Help on New Health Plan." *Los Angeles Times,* January 22.

Rosenthal, A.M. 1994. "The First Ladyship." *New York Times*, March 11, Sec. A.

Ryden, Patricia. 1993. "A Feminist Analysis of the Constructed Role of First Lady: Hillary Rodham Clinton as First Citizen." Paper presented at the Speech Communication Association Annual Meeting, New Orleans.

Safire, William. 1996. "Blizzard of Lies." *New York Times*, January 8, Sec. A.

Sapiro, Virginia. 1983. *The Political Integration of Women.* Urbana: The University of Illinois Press.

Sapiro, Virginia and Pamela Conover. 1993. "Gender in the 1992 Electorate." Unpublished paper.

Sheehy, Gail. 1992. "What Hillary Wants." *Vanity Fair*, May: 142-47, 212-17.

Shepard, Alicia C. 1994. "The Second Time Around." *American Journalism Review,* June: 29-34.

Sherrill, Martha. 1992. "A Clinton In the Cabinet?" *Washington Post*, December 19.

Sims, Anastatia. 1995. "Beyond the Ballot: The Radical Vision of the Antisuffragists." In *Votes for Women.* Ed. Marjoie Spruill Wheeler. Knoxville: University of Tennessee Press.

Simsbury, Robert. 1996. "Cherie Will Be No Hillary Clinton, Says Labour Leader." *The Daily Telegraph*, April 10, Sec. A1.

Stuckey, Mary. 1993. "Hillary Clinton as a Cultural Icon." Roundtable paper presented at the annual meeting of the Southern Political Science Association, Savannah, Georgia.

Tenpas, Kathleen. 1996. "Women on the White House Staff: A Longitudinal Analysis (1939-1994)." In *The Other Elites: Women, Politics, and Power in the Executive Branch.* Ed. Janet Martin and Maryanne Borrelli. New York: Lynne Reiner.

Toner, Robin. 1992. "Backlash for Hillary Clinton Puts Negative Image to Rout." *New York Times*, September 24, Sec. A.

Tyler, Patrick E. 1995. "Hillary Clinton in China Details Abuse of Women." *New York Times*, September 6, Sec. A1.

Walsh, Kenneth. 1993. "Now the First Chief Advocate," *U.S. News & World Report*, January 25: 46-50.

Walsh, Kenneth, Matthew Cooper, and Gloria Borger. 1994. "Taking Their Measure." *U.S. News & World Report*, January 31: 42-48.

Woodward, Bob. 1994. *The Agenda: Inside the Clinton White House.* New York: Simon & Schuster.

Wooten, Jim. 1992. "Hillary Clinton, Tammy Wynette: Both are Winners." *Atlanta Journal and Constitution*, February 2: C.

Zabarenko, Deborah. 1992. "Stand by Your Man? New Look in Campaign Wives." Reuters. February 4.

Index

Adams, Abigail, 5, 15-17
accountability, 23, 113, 141, 142
age and support, 38, 39, 63, 64, 70-73, 75, 106
American National Election Study (ANES), 36-41, 43, 57, 72, 74, 75, 82
Aristotle, 9, 10
Blair, Tony, 133
Bush, Barbara, 19, 28, 29, 33, 34, 42, 43, 79, 80, 84, 93, 94, 96, 97, 138, 144
Carter, Rosalynn, 15-18, 22, 79, 83, 85, 87, 93, 107, 152
Clinton, Bill, 25, 29, 30, 33, 34, 36, 41, 72-77, 82, 88, 100, 102-106, 108, 109, 112, 117, 118, 125, 127
Clinton, Hillary Rodham, 3-8, 15-34, 36, 37, 40-42, 45, 51, 55, 58, 59, 62-64, 66, 70, 72, 73, 78, 82, 83, 87, 88, 95-97, 100, 101, 106-108, 110-114, 117-119, 121, 126, 129-137, 144, 145, 155, 156
  and 1992 campaign, 34, 36, 45, 100, 119
  Health Care Task Force, 6, 7, 20, 97, 107-112, 114, 130, 136, 144
  media, 5, 6, 22, 25-30, 32, 36, 40, 55, 59, 73, 96, 97, 100, 113, 114, 117, 126, 132, 137
  personal qualities, 6, 110, 119
  popularity, 19, 45, 51, 59, 62, 82, 101, 131, 136, 137
  as presidential advisor, 141
  and support, 7, 13, 14, 16, 24, 29, 31, 33, 36, 38, 39, 54, 55, 59, 62-64, 66, 70, 71, 73, 75, 76, 83, 85, 100, 101, 104, 106-108, 110, 113, 117, 136, 137, 145, 149, 154
  Whitewater, 6, 7, 55, 64, 82, 100, 110, 113, 114, 118, 126, 129, 130, 132, 133, 136
Democrats, 38, 39, 57, 63, 66, 70, 78, 105, 124, 130, 137, 147
Dukakis, Kitty, 30, 34, 42, 85
feminism, 4, 19, 30, 43, 119, 135, 139
Harding, Florence, 16
Health Care Task Force, 6, 7, 20, 97, 107-112,

114, 130, 136, 137, 142, 144

Johnson, Lady Bird, 15, 24, 92, 150

Kennedy, Jacqueline, 78, 85

Lincoln, Mary Todd, 17

Madison Guaranty, 7, 132

media coverage, 26, 126

National Organization for Women, 13

Nixon, Pat, 14, 78

Nixon, Richard, 30, 100

Office of the First Lady, 91, 93, 115, 140

Polk, Sarah, 16, 17, 24

public opinion polls, 6, 23, 82, 135, 137

race and support, 38, 39, 63, 64, 71, 73, 75, 104, 106

Reagan, Nancy, 32, 34, 36, 79, 80, 93, 94, 96, 97

Republicans, 10, 12, 15, 27, 30, 39, 66, 71, 72, 105-107, 125, 141, 144

Rose Law Firm, 25, 125

Seneca Falls, 11

sex and support, 38, 39, 64, 66, 70, 73, 75, 76, 104, 106

Southern Focus Poll, 62, 74, 75, 84

staff, 16, 17, 24, 40, 89, 91-96, 100, 115, 130, 132, 140-144, 156

Stanton, Elizabeth Cady, 11

suffrage/suffragists, 11, 12, 24, 148, 153

Taft, Helen, 16

Travel office, 17, 132, 133, 152

Whitewater, 6, 7, 55, 64, 82, 100, 110, 113, 114, 118, 120, 125-130, 132, 133, 136

Wilson, Edith, 92

Wilson, Ellen, 17

Wynette, Tammy, 26, 31, 157